MURDER & MAYHEM
IN CHICAGO'S
VICE DISTRICTS

TROY TAYLOR

Charleston — London

THE
History
PRESS

Published by The History Press
Charleston, SC 29403
www.historypress.net

Copyright © 2009 by Troy Taylor
All rights reserved

First published 2009

Manufactured in the United States

ISBN 978.1.59629.692.3

Library of Congress CIP data applied for.

CONTENTS

Acknowledgements

I would like to thank Adam Selzer and John Winterbauer for their continued inspiration, as well as my friend Ken Berg, who is the expert on sex and deviancy in Chicago (and I mean that in a nice way). Thanks also to Karen Abbott and the many other writers and chroniclers of vice in the Windy City, especially Herbert Asbury and Richard Lindberg. Thanks also to Jonathan Simcosky at The History Press and to Haven Taylor, who always encouraged me to try something outside of my usual box.

INTRODUCTION

C hicago was created by blood, fire, sin and unbridled perseverance. The early residents came to an unlikely place, a swampy wasteland on the edge of a lake, and began to build a settlement that endured through Indian massacres, fires and civil unrest.

The city was almost destroyed before it even had a chance to begin. The first settlers were wiped out in the midst of the War of 1812, during the Fort Dearborn Massacre. Originally, the fort had offered shelter and protection to those who braved the daunting wilderness, but as tensions among the Native American tribes began to rise at the start of the war, it became clear that the protection the fort offered was merely an illusion. After orders came from the American military command to abandon Fort Dearborn, the commanders reached an uneasy truce with the Indians that would allow them safe passage to Indiana. As a column of soldiers and civilians, including women and children, traveled along the shore of Lake Michigan, however, the Native Americans attacked and killed 148 of the settlers and soldiers. Those who survived but did not escape were tortured throughout the night. Fort Dearborn was burned to the ground but was later rebuilt after the war. By then, more settlers had arrived at what would someday be Chicago, eager to lay claim to a region where no city should have ever been built.

At that time, Chicago was merely a collection of wooden cabins, a place that was of little interest to travelers and new arrivals. A visitor in 1823 noted:

The village presents no cheering prospect...it consists of a few huts, inhabited by a miserable race of men, scarcely equal to the Indians from whom they are descended. Their log and bark houses are low, filthy and disgusting, displaying not the least trace of comfort.

Not surprisingly, Chicago grew slowly, and by 1832, it had swelled to a population of only about five hundred souls. In was in this year that the Blackhawk War, an Indian uprising, broke out in Illinois. The existence of Chicago was threatened again, not by Native Americans, but by smallpox.

Hundreds of soldiers arrived in the settlement in the spring of 1832 and found that there was little room, and little food, for the military men and the residents of the community. When General Winfield Scott arrived with hundreds of additional soldiers in July, the situation became even worse because he also brought a smallpox epidemic with him. The Indian peril was quickly forgotten. The townspeople and the newly arrived settlers quickly took flight, emptying Chicago of its civilian population. Only the military men remained, compelled by orders and a sense of duty, and they spent three weeks fighting the epidemic and digging hasty graves for those who died. By autumn, the war had ended, and the soldiers and the smallpox departed. The townspeople returned to their homes, and life in Chicago resumed.

The soldiers who caused so many problems for Chicago were also largely responsible for the city's early growth. The men who had been forced on an excursion through the wilderness of northern Illinois returned to the East with marvelous tales of the area's beauty and of the forests, mill sites and farmland that was waiting for the arrival of settlers. In scores of eastern communities, these reports were heard with great interest, and soon homesteaders began traveling to Illinois and to Chicago.

The first wave of the tide of immigration reached Chicago in the spring of 1833. Most settlers passed through the city on their way to other places, but some, attracted by the city's potential, ended their journey there. Chicago was a city of wooden huts in 1833, with only one frame building, the warehouse of George W. Dole. However, that summer was a time of great activity, and dozens of frame homes and structures were built. They were of flimsy and haphazard construction, to be sure, but their presence provided convincing evidence that civilization was coming to the shores of Lake Michigan. And with civilization came vice.

Even from these early days, Chicago thrived on its reputation for being a wide-open town. The city gained notoriety for its promotion of vice in

An early view of Chicago shows the second Fort Dearborn, which was constructed before the Civil War. The soldiers from the fort, and those who arrived during the war, played an important role in the creation of organized vice districts in Chicago. *Courtesy of the Chicago Historical Society.*

every shape and form. It embraced the arrival of prostitutes, gamblers, grifters and an outright criminal element. A commercialized form of vice flourished less than two decades later, during the Civil War era, and it is believed that more than one thousand prostitutes roamed the dark evening streets of Chicago. Randolph Street was lined with bordellos, wine rooms and cheap dance halls, and the area became known as Gambler's Row, mostly because a man gambled with his life when braving the streets of this seedy and dangerous district.

Most of the gambling in early Chicago was betting on frequent horse races, which were promoted by prominent settler "Jolly Mark" Beaubien, and other local sports. There was plenty of friendly card playing going on in taverns and private homes, but there were also a few games conducted by professionals who had drifted into town from St. Louis and eastern cities. Little is known about these cardsharps, but their activities were extensive enough to incur the wrath of the religious element in the community and make them the object of Chicago's first moral reform.

The attempt to drive out the gamblers was led by Reverend Jeremiah Porter, founder of Chicago's first regularly organized church, the First Presbyterian. Reverend Porter lived in New Jersey for many years after leaving the Princeton Theological Seminary and came to the West in late 1831 as chaplain to the garrison at Fort Brady in Michigan. He stayed in Sault Ste. Marie for about a year and a half with great success, managing to stop the dancing to which soldiers and settlers had been accustomed in order to relieve the boredom of the winter months and converting to religion and temperance every person in the fort and settlement except for a young lieutenant and his wife. The couple stayed outside of the fold, despite almost constant prayer and ministering.

Early in 1833, when troops from Fort Brady were sent to Chicago to relieve the garrison at Fort Dearborn, Reverend Porter accompanied them. He arrived on May 13 and less than one week later delivered his first sermon in the carpenter shop of the fort. He soon organized a congregation of twenty-six members, and on July 7, 1833, he held the first communion service ever celebrated in Chicago. Plans were made to build a church, and a lot was purchased at Clark and Lake Streets, which was, in those times, according to Herbert Asbury in *Gem of the Prairie*, "a lonely spot, almost inaccessible on account of surrounding sloughs and bogs." Materials for the church were assembled, but before actual work could begin, squatters started to erect a building on the Lake Street side of the property. When confronted, they refused to leave. Instead of turning the other cheek, the outraged Presbyterians went to the site at night, attached heavy chains to the building, hitched a team of oxen to the chains and dragged the structure two hundred yards down Lake Street. The members of the congregation then went to work with hammers and saws on their own building. The church was completed soon after.

With a church building well underway, Reverend Porter turned his attention to the gamblers who had infested the settlement. Many complaints had been made about these men, mostly on the grounds that they were luring young men to perdition. Several powerful sermons so aroused the authorities that two gambling dens were raided and two card players were placed in jail for two days, while others were warned that they must obey the law and close down their establishments.

Gambling in Chicago was curbed but not for long. In December 1833, a letter to the *Chicago Democrat* declared that gambling was more prevalent than ever, and Reverend Porter returned to the attack. In 1834, a mass meeting of the antigambling faction appointed a Committee of Nine to devise measures for stopping gambling and punishments for gamblers. Resolutions by the committee pledged its members to "withhold the hand of friendship" from card players and to wage unrelenting warfare on anyone who dared bring

The Reverend Jeremiah Porter, Chicago's first reformer to speak out against vice.

games of chance into the city. The committee's report stated, "Cost what it may, we are determined to root out this vice, and to hunt down those who gain by its infamous substance." Reverend Porter launched another campaign in the summer of 1835, and during this rousing "season of prayer," many young men were converted to the Lord and two gamblers were imprisoned.

The gamblers, however, were not especially disturbed by Reverend Porter or by the pronouncements of the Committee of Nine, especially since the minister abandoned the fight soon after the "season of prayer" and resigned his position to accept a call to Peoria. The gamblers knew that mere words and proclamations could never hurt them, and with the immigration boom that was coming to the region, city officials were going to be too busy to worry about the few dollars that foolish residents were losing at the gaming tables. Consequently, the games became larger, and more and more gamblers began flocking to Chicago.

By the early 1840s, Chicago was home to more gambling houses than either St. Louis or Cincinnati, and it was the most important gaming center north of New Orleans and west of the Allegheny Mountains. Short card games like poker were principally played, with sometimes an occasional faro table in more upscale spots. Roulette, keno and craps were largely unknown until after 1850, and betting on horses remained a favorite Chicago pastime.

Most of the Chicago gamblers of this period had been kicked out of Natchez and Vicksburg during an uprising against cardsharps in the Mississippi River Valley in 1835. Virtually all of them had learned their trade on the Mississippi River steamboats. Among them were sporting men like John Sears, George Rhodes, Walt Winchester, Cole Martin, "King Cole" Conant and the Smith brothers—Charles, Montague and "One-Lung" George. The largest figure of this group in Chicago history was John Sears, a southerner of French descent who was one of the most expert poker players of the time. But even more than for his skill at cards, Sears was known for his love of poetry, especially that of Burns and Shakespeare, for his gift of storytelling and for his good looks and lavish wardrobe. For years, he was considered the best-dressed man in Chicago.

As in other American frontier towns, the gamblers were followed to Chicago by the prostitutes and their pimps. As early as 1835, the town's board of trustees adopted an ordinance that imposed a fine of twenty-five dollars on any person convicted of keeping a house of ill repute. Less than three years later, in February 1838, another ordinance made the fine even higher. At the same time, a complaint was made to the authorities that brothels were in operation on Wells Street, between Jackson and First—shabby, poorly kept little dives, but the beginnings of the largest red-light district that the United States had ever seen. They were also the first of the resorts to make Wells Street such a fearsome place that in 1870 the board of aldermen changed the name of the street to Fifth Avenue so that it might no longer dishonor Captain William Wells, the frontier hero for whom it had been named. It was not changed back to Wells until after the turn of the twentieth century.

Close on the heels of the gamblers and whores, the fundamental props of the underworld and vice districts, came the ragtag hoodlums, con men, pickpockets, burglars, gunmen, thieves and counterfeiters. To satisfy the demand created by these unsavory arrivals, more saloons were opened, and liquor flowed in Chicago like never before. Taverns and saloons became so numerous and disposed of such quantities of bad liquor that the city, which had only just become an official municipality, was already earning a national reputation as a tough town. John Hawkins, head of a national temperance movement that was based in Washington, said that he "could frankly state that in all his tours of the United States, he had never seen a town which seemed so like the universal grog-shop as did Chicago."

By the 1840s, Chicago newspapers were publishing an increasing number of stories about thievery, holdups, disturbances by drunken men, street fights and minor riots and were complaining that the liquor stores and taverns were frequented by "rowdies, blacklegs and other species of loafers." A newspaper in Jackson, Michigan, wrote that "the population of Chicago is said to be principally composed of dogs and loafers." One newspaper, the *Chicago American*, agreed and published a warning:

> *The scoundrel that set fire the other night to the old post office building is suspected. He and all other suspicious loafers about the city had better, as soon as possible, make themselves scarce, or the city watch will be at their heels.*

If the editors of the newspaper had known each of the "loafers" in the city personally, it is likely that their hints of reprisal would have been directed toward a young Irishman named John Stone, who had arrived in America at the age of thirteen and just over twenty years later was hanged on the gallows in the first legal execution in Chicago history.

Stone arrived in Chicago in late 1838, after having served prison sentences in Canada for robbery and murder and in New York for stealing horses. He worked odd jobs, mostly as a woodcutter, but spent most of his time in saloons and in Chicago's first billiard hall, which was opened in 1836 on the second floor of Couch's tavern, the first Tremont House, at Lake and Dearborn Streets. In the spring of 1840, Stone was arrested for the rape and murder of Mrs. Lucretia Thompson, the wife of a Cook County farmer.

The evidence against Stone was damning. A piece of flannel torn from a shirt that belonged to him was found next to the body of the victim. He was also found burning the rest of his clothes, and a club that still had Mrs. Thompson's hair and blood on it was discovered in his possession. A witness during the trial also recalled that Stone had threatened her and had apparently made a sexual remark to her, "threatening her virtue." All of this was enough to get him convicted of first-degree murder. A newspaper stated, "Nor has there been any doubt of its justice, although John Stone stolidly asserted his innocence to the last."

On Friday, July 10, 1840, bound in chains, Stone was placed in a wagon and, escorted by two hundred mounted citizens and sixty armed militiamen who were commanded by Colonel Seth Johnson, taken to a spot on the lakeshore about three miles from the courthouse. There, he was hanged by a large and rowdy group of spectators. Stone continued to proclaim his innocence. He swore that he had never entered the Thompson home and that he had not seen her on the day she died. He also stated that he believed two individuals were engaged in the murder, but when asked if he knew them, he said that he would hang before their blood would be on his hands.

Stone was attended on the gallows by Reverend Hallam, Isaac R. Gavin, Deputies Davis and Lowe and the sheriff, who seemed particularly affected by the hanging, to the point of tears. After a prayer was offered by Reverend Hallam, the death warrant was read and a cap was pulled down over the face of the prisoner. Stone plunged to his doom from a height of only four feet and was slowly strangled to death. His corpse was hauled away in a wagon and was given over to Drs. Boone and Dyer for dissection.

It was a grim and painful death for the city's first executed murderer, a man who had gained his infamy among the saloons, brothels and pool halls of Chicago's first vice district.

WHEN THE CITY WENT TO WAR OVER BEER

O ne of the strangest incidents to occur in the history of old Chicago was the infamous Lager Beer Riot of 1855. It was an event that would test not only the city's government but also the fledging police force. It came about because of prejudice, fierce independence and a city's thirst for beer.

As crime began to wreak havoc on the city in the mid-1800s, it came to the realization of many that the police officers who had been hired to offer protection to the citizens were hardly better than the criminals themselves. The Chicago Police Department has been plagued for many years by allegations of corruption and graft—allegations that were well deserved during the turbulent years of Prohibition—but in the early years of the city, the complaints about the police force were mostly due to a lack of confidence in their abilities. The job requirements for law enforcement positions were rudimentary at best, and it was necessary for the policemen on the beat to be tough. For this reason, other problems were often overlooked in favor of brutality. The behavior of many officers, which ranged from bribe taking to covert alliances with criminals, generated public mistrust of policemen at large. Undoubtedly, there were many brave, upstanding and conscientious men in the ranks, but a bad reputation was earned for the force by the men who were inclined toward violence or eager for a handout. The good men on the police force often faced an uphill battle against crime in the city.

Chicago had no peace officer of any kind until the fall of 1825, when Archibald Clybourne, a native of Virginia and one of the founders of Chicago's meatpacking industry, was appointed the constable of Peoria

County, a huge wilderness tract that included all of northeastern Illinois. There is no way that any one person could have possibly patrolled this entire region, even though the white population of the area amounted to fewer than one hundred people at the time. The records say that Clybourne never made an arrest, and his official duties consisted of little more than attending the frontier courts and serving documents that were produced by justices of the peace.

There is no mention of a police official in the roster of town officials at the time of the first municipal election in 1833 and nothing to indicate that there was a police force of any kind for another two years. The peace in the settlement was kept by Constable Reed and a mysterious figure referred to in historical records only as "Officer Beach," who carried the keys to the jail. Crime was discouraged by the placement of signs and placards at prominent street corners notifying residents that violations of law were punishable by fines and that half of the fine would be paid to those who informed on the lawbreakers. Those unable to pay their fines were fitted with a ball and chain and were forced to work on the streets for various lengths of time.

The city's first policeman was O. Morrison, about whom nothing is known, save for the fact that he was elected to the position in 1835 and again in 1836. In 1837, John Shrigley was elected high constable, an office that was created when Chicago became a city. Samuel J. Low took over the position (also called chief of the city watch) in 1839, and three assistants were appointed, although the city charter allowed for as many as six. This same type of organization was maintained over the next fifteen years, when Chicago's police force never numbered more than nine men. Needless to say, the officers were greatly outnumbered by the population of the city, which ranged from forty-five hundred to nearly eighty thousand people during that same time period. Is it any wonder that Chicago gained its reputation as a wide-open town?

It was impossible for such a small body of men to watch over the entire city, yet Chicago had nothing better than the constable and watchmen system until 1855, when the city council adopted ordinances that created an actual police department. Cyrus P. Bradley, a prominent volunteer fireman and later a famous private detective and member of the Secret Service, was appointed as the first chief of police. Three precincts were formed, stations were established and about eighty officers were hired. These officers had no insignia to designate their positions until 1857, when Mayor John Wentworth issued leather stars and allowed the officers to carry heavy canes in daytime and batons at night. Each man was also equipped with a "creaker," a sort of loud rattle that was later replaced by a whistle. In 1858, Mayor John Haines changed the leather star to brass and introduced the first uniform, which was a blue frock coat and a blue hat with a gold band. He also hired another twenty men.

Chicago's new police force received its baptism of fire during the infamous Lager Beer Riot in 1855, the city's first serious disturbance.

In the early 1850s, a wave of sentiment that claimed to be patriotic swept the country, and out of this came the Know-Nothing political party. Its slogan was "Put none but Americans on guard," meaning that only native-born Americans could serve on the police force and in politics. Dr. Levi Day Boone, grandnephew of famous Indian fighter Daniel Boone, was the head of the Know-Nothing Party in Chicago and somehow managed to get himself elected mayor, despite the fact that the city was made up of mostly Irish and German immigrants.

He implemented his new political policy and demanded that all applicants for city employment, especially those on the new police force, be able to prove that they were born on American soil. Many in Chicago were angry with this, but not as angry as they were about the enforcement of the old (but seldom used) law that forced saloons to be closed on Sundays. This might have still been acceptable if not for Boone's peculiar manner of enforcing it. Only beer halls, which were mainly located on the North Side with its German population, would be closed. Saloons that sold whiskey, on the South Side, could remain open. Boone also recommended that annual licensing fees for beer halls be raised from $50 to $300.

The owners of the German beer halls and beer gardens refused to close, and they refused to pay the higher fee. More than two hundred people were arrested and put on trial. The hearing was scheduled for April 21, 1855, but on that morning, a mob of more than four hundred Germans marched on the courthouse. Their representatives entered the courtroom and announced to Judge Henry C. Rucker that if any of the defendants were found guilty, a riot would commence. The mob then left the courthouse and stopped all traffic on Randolph and Clark Streets until a legion of police officers could be summoned. The officers, led by Captain of Police Luther Nichols, charged into the mob with clubs, causing the Germans to break ranks and run. Shots were fired, but no one was injured.

Meanwhile, the mob retreated to the North Side to make new plans. It returned to the area around the courthouse that afternoon with over 1,000 men, who had armed themselves with shotguns, rifles, pistols, clubs, butcher knives and hammers. Mayor Boone countered this by bringing every police officer in town to the area, plus about 150 deputies. He even ordered that cannons be brought to the courthouse.

The rioters marched on the Clark Street Bridge, and as they approached it, the mayor ordered that the bridge be opened so that the group would be unable to cross. Mob members shouted and yelled until (for some inexplicable reason) the bridge was put back into place. They swarmed across the river and collided with the police officers on the other side. Shots were fired and knives flashed—all for the right to drink beer on Sunday! The pitched battle lasted for almost an hour, and a number of injuries were later reported, along with a single death. One of the Germans, Peter Martin, fired a shotgun, and Patrolman George Hunt lost his arm from the blast. Martin was then killed where he stood. Rumor persisted for some time that more than one man was killed, but this was never confirmed, as the Germans were closemouthed about their injuries and fatalities. Hunt was later arrested for the murder but was soon released and given a $3,000 reward by the city council.

In the end, sixty people were arrested for their part in the Lager Beer Riot but only fourteen were tried and only two were found guilty of anything. They were later granted new trials, but nothing ever came of it.

Eventually, the story faded away into memory—just as the Know-Nothing Party did. Boone lost his bid for reelection, and two months after the riot, the voters soundly defeated a prohibition law in Chicago.

BEFORE THE GREAT FIRE

CHICAGO'S EARLY VICE DISTRICTS

By the late 1850s, Chicago was able to boast almost fifteen hundred businesses within its borders, dozens of banks, railroad lines, millions of dollars' worth of imports and exports, forty newspapers and periodicals, a half dozen theatres, eighty ballrooms "where bands played from morning to night" and a still-growing population of more than ninety-three thousand people. But not all of Chicago's accomplishments were ones to be proud of. Crime of every description had increased dramatically in just two decades, and a national bank panic was spreading throughout the country, causing businesses to fail and widespread unemployment in the Windy City. This led to burglaries, shootings and holdups by bands of young men who had once been respectable laborers. They were driven, according to one lurid newspaper account, "from sheer want and by the sufferings of their families to try their fortunes as garrotters, highwaymen, burglars and thieves."

The newspapers published daily accounts of these criminals and offered almost hysterical warnings of even worse things to come. Author John J. Flinn wrote in 1891:

> *The people became almost panic-stricken and honest citizens returning to their homes or visiting friends after dark, ran the risk of being mistaken for criminals and shot. Life and property were in constant danger from mobs of criminals.*

One of the squalid brothels of early Chicago. The Great Fire wiped out the worst of these run-down and seedy establishments, although even worse houses soon took their place.

After noting that fifty-three burglaries had been reported in one week, the *Chicago Tribune* declared that Chicago was "at the mercy of the criminal classes" and called for citizens' groups to employ Allan Pinkerton and his detectives to clean up the city. This was never done, but a group of businessmen did hire Pinkerton to stop a gang of grave robbers who were raiding the Old Catholic Burying Ground north of the city, opening the graves and selling the bodies to medical students. Eight operatives guarded the cemetery for weeks.

But incidents of thievery and murder were not the real scourge of Chicago crime—and certainly not where questionable fortunes were being made. The real problems came from the vice and red-light districts, many of which have become legendary in Chicago history.

The small group of gambling joints that could once be found in Chicago had become, by the late 1850s, a large and festering colony of skinning joints with a few square houses struggling to survive. The liquor stores had given way to cheap hotels and dingy saloons with backrooms that had become the lairs of thieves and hoodlums. The few brothels on Wells Street had spawned a score of such establishments. Most of them were two-bits houses catering exclusively to the working man, but a few of them charged from fifty cents to a dollar, had carpets on the floor and pianos in the parlor and advertised with red lights and red window curtains. The most pretentious houses, though in no way equal to the luxurious parlor houses that were still to come, included Julia Davenport's Green House on State Street and the Prairie Queen, also on State Street, kept by Eleanor Herrick, a fixture in Chicago's red-light district for more than thirty years. The Prairie Queen was famous for the variety of its entertainment, offering dancing every night, an erotic show once a week and a monthly prizefight between two bare knucklers, who fought for a two-dollar purse and a night with one of Eleanor Herrick's girls. The police ignored the dancing and sex shows but finally stopped the prizefighting when they raided the Prairie Queen on June 3, 1857. Billy Fagan, a local tough, and Con McCarthy, a fighter from Rochester, New York, were both taken into custody.

In addition to those on Wells and State Streets, brothels of varying degrees of filth had appeared on Blue Island Avenue and on Madison, Monroe and Green Streets. There was a particularly depraved whorehouse on the second floor of a brick warehouse at number 109 South Water Street that housed a large number of prostitutes and had rows of cribs that were rented to streetwalkers. The police had often raided the place to quell drunken orgies, but on the night of October 19, 1857, they arrived too late. An intoxicated harlot had kicked over a lighted lamp, and in the blaze that followed, twenty-three people lost their lives and the warehouse was completely destroyed. All of the prostitutes escaped with their lives, however.

But even the worst of these dives was a veritable palace when compared with those of the Sands, one of the earliest vice districts in the city. It was described as the "vilest and most dangerous place in Chicago" by the *Chicago Tribune*, and by 1857, it consisted of a few dozen ramshackle buildings, each housing gambling parlors, saloons and brothels, in which a charge for services ranged from twenty-five to fifty cents. Originally, the area, which was located on a stretch of lakeshore just north of the Chicago River, catered mostly to sailors and canal men, but it later expanded into a resort area and a hiding place for all manner of criminals.

The leaders of this unsavory community were Dutch Frank, who ran dogfights; Freddy Webster; Anna Wilson; Mike O'Brien, a burglar and former fighter, and his son, Mike, a pickpocket and pimp for his four sisters; and John Hill and his wife, Mary. The Hills were said to be the first couple in Chicago to work the "badger game," an old-time sex swindle in which a woman picks up a man and brings him home. Her husband then "accidentally" comes in and catches them in the act, demanding satisfaction from the man, which comes in the form of the sucker's money. Unfortunately, John Hill had a wide jealous streak, and after every con, he always tried to kill his wife for encouraging the victim in the racket to get into bed with her.

Freddy Webster owned a brothel that was incredibly vicious, even for the Sands. One of his girls, Margaret McGinness, was said to have been neither sober nor out of the house for five years; she was also said not to have had her clothes on for three. She customarily entertained between ten and forty men each night. She died in March 1857 from alcoholism, and hers was the seventh unnatural death in the Sands that week.

Anna Wilson's brothel, the only fifty-cent house in the Sands, was famous for the presence of a belligerent young whore named Annie Stafford, also known as Gentle Annie—a nickname that was meant as a joke. Annie had a terrific reputation as a brutal fighter, and she was Madam Wilson's chief weapon in her war with Eleanor Herrick of the Prairie Queen. The battle began early in 1857 when Herrick lured away one of Wilson's prettiest girls by offering her a clean dress and more money. The madams and their loyal girls fought several indecisive street battles, but on the night of April 3, Gentle Annie, supported by three more of Wilson's girls and several pimps, made a surprise attack on the Prairie Queen. They broke down the front door with clubs, smashed the furniture, chased away the customers and then gave Madam Herrick and a half dozen of her girls sound thrashings. Gentle Annie then returned to the Sands, bringing with her the wayward harlot who had started all of the trouble in the first place.

The Sands came to an end during a period of violence that marked the tenure of Mayor "Long John" Wentworth. He was undoubtedly the most colorful of all of Chicago's mayors. During his tenure in office, he fired the entire city police force, personally caught and arrested gamblers, tore down advertising signs that personally offended him and illegally leveled an entire neighborhood. He definitely made an impression on the city of Chicago, and if that impression had been any greater, the city might not have survived his term in office.

Wentworth was twenty-one when he arrived barefoot in Chicago. It was October 1836, and the young man had almost nothing to his name. Somehow, though, within four weeks he was the owner of the local newspaper, and by age twenty-eight, he was in Congress. He soon was offered his first bribe—by the people of Wisconsin. They badly wanted to become a state but needed the population of Chicago to do so. They told Wentworth that if he would vote to have the boundaries of Wisconsin

One of Chicago's most unusual mayors, "Long John" Wentworth was almost singlehandedly responsible for the destruction of the Sands vice district. *Courtesy of the Chicago Historical Society.*

redrawn to the southern tip of Lake Michigan, swallowing up Chicago, they would make him their first senator. Wentworth refused, having no interest in becoming a citizen of Wisconsin.

"Long John" certainly earned his nickname. He stood six feet, six inches tall and weighed over three hundred pounds. He would usually order as many as thirty courses for a single dinner and would insist that everything, from soup to dessert, be placed on the table before him when he was ready to eat. He always sat alone at a table that had been made for four or five diners and would spin the table around so that whatever dish he wanted to eat from next was within reach.

He became mayor of Chicago in March 1857, taking office after a violent campaign that saw one man killed and several others wounded near polling places. Early in his administration, he decided that he didn't like low-hanging advertising signs because he constantly bumped his head on them. He declared that they should be removed. On June 18, 1857, he gathered all of the police officers and express drivers in the city and prepared them for their mission by personally pouring them all shots of bourbon. He then ordered them to remove "every swinging sign, awning post or box found protruding two feet or more beyond the front of buildings." All of the signs were thrown into a large pile on State Street, and their owners were allowed to retrieve them if they wished—and to hang them somewhere else.

This was not the only time that Wentworth created his own laws, and it was certainly not the last time he personally enforced them. One night, Wentworth went along with police officers on a raid of Burrough's Place, a notorious gambling den. When the police arrived, the owners sounded an alarm, and the fleeing customers ran out the front door and into the clutches of the city's enormous mayor. Wentworth personally supervised the booking of eighteen of the prisoners who were captured that night. Later, the establishment's lawyer, a man named Charlie Cameron, appeared at the jail and demanded to speak to his clients. His request was denied, so he crept around to the back of the building and whispered through the barred window. Enraged, Wentworth grabbed the attorney and locked him up, too. Police returned to the gambling parlor and stripped the place, and Burrough's never reopened.

Even though Chicagoans were concerned about gambling and vice in their city, many began to question Wentworth's authority, especially when it concerned the police force. The mayor was so busy making arrests, writing laws and designing uniforms and badges that many had to wonder how he was managing to run the city. Wentworth had overstepped his bounds, many believed, and so local citizens convinced the state legislature to create a board of three police commissioners to take control of the Chicago police force out of the mayor's hands.

Undaunted, Wentworth decided to fire the entire police force in protest. On March 26, 1861, the force was assembled in the courthouse, and Wentworth discharged the officers from duty, leaving the streets unprotected and the stations empty and abandoned. Of course, it was all done for effect. Wentworth had left custodians in all of the police stations and had told the men to be ready to be called to action if the town bells were sounded. Symbolically, though, Chicago had been turned over to the criminals.

How long the city was actually unprotected is open to debate. Some say that it was for as short a time as twelve hours, while others say that thirty-six hours passed before the police board began to rehire the officers. However, there are those who say that the old police force was so inept that no one ever knew the difference.

One of the most famous statements that Wentworth ever made during his tenure occurred during Chicago's first royal visit. The distinguished guest was the prince of Wales, who later became King Edward VII. When the prince came to Chicago in 1860, Wentworth introduced the royal guest from a hotel balcony to a crowd gathered on the street. He slapped the prince on the back and said, "Boys, this is the prince of Wales. He's come to see the city, and I'm going to show him around. Prince, these are the boys!"

But Wentworth's ego knew no bounds, even when it came to the heir to the throne. When asked how he felt about sitting next to the future king of England, Wentworth corrected the interrogator by saying, "I was not sitting beside the prince. He sat beside me." One author once submitted a new history of Chicago to Wentworth for his approval, and the mayor scratched out all of the entries in the book that did not pertain to him and handed it back. "There is a correct history of the city," he reportedly said.

Wentworth was even full of himself when it came to his death. Before he died, he bought a huge burial plot at Rosehill Cemetery that took up nearly two-thirds of an acre. He died on October 16, 1888, and was buried beneath a seventy-foot monument of his own design. It remains the largest in the cemetery and for years had no inscription on it. When he was asked about this peculiarity, he replied that if nothing was placed on the stone, people would ask whose monument it was. When told, they would "ransack the libraries to find out who John Wentworth was." But few libraries were actually ransacked, so his name and a list of accomplishments were eventually added to the stone.

In 1857, when his plans to clean up the city were at their peak, Wentworth's schemes went beyond simply closing a gambling den, and he decided to level the entire Sands vice district. Long before Wentworth was elected mayor, there had been talk of demolishing the haphazard shacks of the Sands, but the land on which they stood was tied up in litigation with the courts. As the *Tribune* explained, "In view of the uncertainty of the law, the litigants were disinclined to take violent measures to eject the occupants." In other words, the landowners were too scared, or were being paid too well, to run the brothel and saloonkeepers off the property. Finally, in April 1857, William B. Ogden bought out several of the landowners, notified the denizens of the Sands to vacate the buildings and also told those who owned their own buildings that he would gladly purchase their shacks. A few sold out, but most of the squatters vowed that they would never leave. This was reported to the mayor, and he promised to take action as soon as he could without risking bloodshed.

The opportunity came during a dogfight between one of Dutch Frank's dogs and an animal owned by Bill Gallagher, a Market Street butcher. The event was to be held at the Brighton racetrack, and on April 20, every able-bodied man in the Sands accompanied Dutch Frank to the scene. Chicago legend has it that Mayor Wentworth may have arranged this fight and caused it to be advertised, but no one really knows for sure. Regardless, he took advantage of it. Dutch Frank and his cohorts had barely left the Sands when Wentworth led a procession of about one hundred well-meaning citizens, a deputy sheriff bearing orders of eviction, thirty or so police officers and a team of horses drawing a wagon that was loaded with hooks and chains. They managed to tear down nine buildings by evening, and by the time darkness was starting to fall, they burned the rest of the district to the ground. When the inhabitants of the Sands returned from the dogfight later that night, the district was in ashes.

On April 21, 1857, the *Chicago Tribune* wrote:

> *Thus this congregation of the vilest haunts of the most depraved and degraded creatures in our city has been literally "wiped out," and the miserable beings who swarmed there driven away. Hereafter, we hope the Sands will be the abode of the honest and the industrious, and that efficient measures will be taken to prevent any other portion of the city from becoming the abode of another such gathering of vile and vicious persons.*

Unfortunately, Wentworth's plan to clean up vice in Chicago backfired. Once the Sands was destroyed, the gamblers, criminals and whores who called the place home simply crossed the Chicago River and, instead of being mostly confined to one small area, spread throughout the city.

During the 1860s, largely due to the helplessness of the Chicago police force, the city acquired a reputation for being "the wickedest city in the United States." Human refuse from all over the United States swarmed into the city. They were drawn to Chicago by the easy money of those boomtown days, as well as the thousands of soldiers on the loose with army payrolls and the knowledge that there was little to fear from the police.

The newcomers took over and enlarged the resorts that had been formed by the refugees from the Sands, and within a year after the start of the Civil War, there was hardly a downtown street that didn't have a row of brothels, saloons, gambling dens and cheap boardinghouses. The criminal class almost wholly occupied the South Side below Madison Street, from the lake to the river, until the Great Fire finally burned them out. The *Chicago Journal* wrote, "We are beset on every side by a gang of desperate villains."

One journalist of the period stated that the "very core of this corruption" was Roger Plant's resort on the northeast corner of Wells and Monroe Streets. Originally, the dive was situated in a single, two-story house, but after one adjoining establishment after another was added on to it, the resort extended about halfway down the block on both streets by the mid-1860s. The police called the place "Roger's Barracks," but Plant referred to it as "Under the Willow," thanks to a lone willow tree that drooped at one corner of the main building, and the name stuck. The appearance of the place was further enhanced by a bright blue shade at each of the windows that bore the words "Why Not?" in gold lettering. This became a catch phrase all over the city.

Under the Willow was described by author Fredrick Francis Cook as "one of the most talked about, if not actually one of the wickedest places on the continent" and as "a refuge for the very nethermost strata of the underworld." It was believed that a tunnel ran from the resort under Wells Street to a number of underground dens located along Wells Street and the south branch of the river. There were at least sixty rooms in the sprawling place, and it offered just about every vice imaginable. The place included a saloon; two or three brothels, where customers were often stripped, robbed and dumped into alleys; rooms for men to meet the ladies of the night; cubicles that were rented to streetwalkers; and hideaways that were used by various species of crooks.

One of Plant's tenants during the Civil War was Mary Hodges, a well-known shoplifter and pickpocket who drove a cart into the shopping district several times a week and returned to the resort with a load of plunder. Another was Mary Brennan, who ran a thieves' school for girls, with two of her own daughters as both pupils and teachers. The children were taught to pick pockets, steal purses and pilfer store counters. They brought all of their loot back to Brennan, who rewarded them with a few pennies to spend on candy. Another tenant of Under the Willow was "Speckled Jimmy" Calwell, a burglar and safecracker who always bound his robbery victims with plaster and tape. He was also believed to have been involved in the building of Chicago's first bomb, which was found on the tracks of the Blue Island horsecar line in late December 1870.

The landlord of the place, Roger Plant, was a diminutive Englishman who only stood an inch above five feet and never weighed more than one hundred pounds. In spite of this, he came to be regarded as a deadly fighter, adept with all kinds of weapons, especially his teeth. Ordinarily, he carried a knife and a gun secreted on his person, but when he got drunk, he would put aside his weapons and ceremoniously drench the willow tree outside with a mixture of whiskey and water. He managed to keep his customers in line, but he was, in turn, dominated by his wife, a huge woman who tipped the scales at nearly three hundred pounds. She was said to frequently tuck her spouse under one arm and spank him with her free hand. Mrs. Plant organized the affairs of the prostitutes in the resort, and when she was not busy with this, she was producing children. No one knows the exact number of children the Plants raised, but it was generally believed to be about fifteen. Each of them learned to pick pockets not long after learning to walk.

Under the Willow operated for about ten years with no interference. In 1868, having made more money than he ever expected, Plant closed the resort, bought a house in the country and began living a respectable life. Several of his children, however, continued to carry on the family business. His son, Roger Jr., was first arrested at the age of fifteen after robbing a Monroe Street saloon. In 1894, when English journalist and reformer W.T. Stead published a black list of Chicago property that was being used for immoral purposes, Roger Plant Jr. was listed as the keeper of three saloons and two brothels, while Kitty and Daisy Plant ran adjoining bordellos on Clark Street.

Chicago also boasted a number of other vice spots that were slightly less vicious than Under the Willow. One of them was John Ryan's Concert Saloon on South Clark Street, which advertised "elegant and chaste performances" but actually presented live sex shows and dancers and became the hangout of some of the city's most dangerous hoodlums. There was also George

Conley's Patch was a slum of cheap saloons, pawnshops, brothels and ramshackle buildings. It would become a casualty of the Great Chicago Fire that was mourned by few people. *Courtesy of* Chicago Today.

Clark's New York Saloon and Ben Sabin's bar, both located on Wells Street. There was also a collection of Negro dives in Shinbone Alley, between Adams and Quincy Streets near Wells, and a huddle of dilapidated old shacks on Chicago Avenue, known as the Chicago Patch. Conley's Patch was a collection of rookeries at Adams and Franklin Streets, and the boss of the area was a gigantic black woman known as the "Bengal Tigress." She became a legend in the Chicago underworld of the era. Her business was procuring young girls for sailors, but she seemed to prefer her leisure time, which she passed fighting, drinking and raising hell. When she went on a drunken rampage, the residents of Conley's Patch locked their doors and windows and waited for the worst to happen. On at least two occasions, the Bengal Tigress singlehandedly tore down several shanties that belonged to occupants who had angered her. The police seldom bothered her, but when they did, they always came in force because it took at least four officers to subdue her and take her into custody.

The Clark Street taverns of Tim Reagan and Andy Routzong, which were noted for the "desperate character of both proprietors and their patrons," were the favorite hangouts of Chicago bounty jumpers during the Civil War. These rowdy individuals enlisted in the army, deserted as soon as they had collected their bounties and then reenlisted under different names in other regiments, repeating the process over and over again. Some of these men operated through bounty brokers, agents who, for a commission, furnished information about what regiments most needed men to fill their quotas and which paid the highest price. Some of them enlisted in as many as a dozen regiments, collecting between $300 and $400 for each enlistment.

The most infamous of the bounty jumpers was a man named Con Brown, a horse thief and robber who had a terrible disposition when drunk but was known for being remarkably kind and generous when sober. Once, after beating a young man, he sobered up and paid his victim's medical bills and gave him a large sum of money besides. During the first three years of the war, Brown got himself on to the roster of no fewer than twenty military units and collected almost $8,000 in bounties. In 1864, while serving a month's sentence at Chicago's Bridewell Prison, he escaped five times with the help of his jailers and enlisted in three different regiments. His crimes finally caught up to him in 1865, and he was sent to the state prison in Joliet. He escaped six times in less than three years. However, prison officials no longer had to worry about him after December 26, 1868—Brown was murdered by Pete Boyle in a saloon in Lemont after he tried to cut Boyle's throat with a knife.

The Chicago vice districts, saloons and brothels thrived during the Civil War, but change was coming, and it would arrive in the form of one of the most devastating fires in American history.

According to legend, the fire was started by a cow in a barn on Chicago's West Side. The animal's owner, a woman named O'Leary, carelessly left a kerosene lantern in the barn after her evening milking, and a cow kicked it over and ignited the hay on the floor. The story started as a rumor and was soon accepted as truth, although history tells a slightly different story.

For several years after the end of the war, a respectable but poor laborer named Patrick O'Leary lived with his family in the three rear rooms of a cottage at 137 De Koven Street on the city's West Side. He lived there with his wife, Catherine, and their five children. The two front rooms of the cottage were rented to the family of Patrick McLaughlin, and on the night of October 8, 1871, the house was a very lively place. The O'Leary family had retired for the evening, but McLaughlin, a fiddler, along with his family and friends, was entertaining his wife's cousin, who had recently

The O'Leary Cottage at 137 De Koven Street. The Great Fire began in the O'Leary barn and devastated the city. *Courtesy of the Chicago Historical Society.*

arrived from Ireland. The rooms were filled with music and drinking, and at some point, a few of the young men went out to get another half gallon of beer—or some milk, depending on who was telling the story.

It is believed that at some point in the evening, some of the McLaughlin clan decided to prepare an oyster stew for their party, and a couple of the young men were sent to get some milk from the cow that the O'Learys stabled in a barn at the rear of the house. A broken lamp found among the ashes of the stable a few days later gave rise to the legend that the cow, or a careless milker, had started the fire that destroyed Chicago.

Late on the evening of October 8, a man named Dennis Sullivan called on the O'Learys and roused Patrick from his bed. The two men chatted for a few minutes, and as Sullivan walked slowly along De Koven Street toward Jefferson, he stopped on the curb to light his pipe. As he raised his head to light the tobacco, shielding his pipe from a strong wind that was blowing, he saw a flicking light in the O'Leary milking barn. Crying an alarm, he rushed into the building and managed to drag out a calf, whose hair had caught fire. But when he went back inside to try and save the horse and cow, his wooden leg caught in a crack between two boards, and he barely escaped with his own life.

This was the beginning of the Great Chicago Fire. Within two hours, it was raging over one hundred acres, devouring the wood-frame homes, barns and buildings and burning wildly out of control. The fire was pushed on by the high winds, the drought-like conditions, the ramshackle wooden structures of the city and the undermanned and poorly equipped fire department. To make matters worse, the firefighters were exhausted, having answered thirty alarms in a week. Only the day before, they had fought for fifteen hours against another blaze on the West Side.

Just before midnight, the fire crossed the Chicago River and spread into the South Side, igniting the roof of a shanty at Adams and Franklin Streets. It then leaped almost at once into the new stables of Frank Parmalee's bus company. Conley's Patch and Shinbone Alley were consumed by fire and smoke, and the prostitutes, pimps and hoodlums ran from the blazing rookeries and joined the crowds of people who were trying to escape. Gambler's Row disappeared. Next, the fire crossed into the business district, destroying stores, hotels, theatres, banks, newspaper offices and public buildings.

Great masses of frightened and now homeless people surged ahead of the flames. They were blistered and scorched by the horrific heat. They carried bundles, babies and invalids, dragging trunks and carts; they stumbled and fell, trampling fallen children, crying and screaming so loudly that sometimes the shouting could be heard above the roar of the flames.

From the burning lairs of the underworld came throngs of gunmen, thieves and prostitutes, hurrying to snatch up the loot that had been left behind or was being carried by the panicked citizens. They roamed together and in packs, taking what they wanted from wagons and carriages and breaking into saloons, stores and homes. They drank liquor, stuffed their pockets with cash and jewelry and covered themselves with fine clothing, rings, necklaces and bracelets. The *Chicago Post* later reported:

> *They smashed windows with their naked hands, regardless of the wounds inflicted, and with bloody fingers rifled till and shelf and cellar, fighting viciously for the spoils of their forage. Women, hollow-eyed and brazen-faced, with filthy drapery tied over them, their clothes in tatters and their feet in trodden-over slippers, moved here and there—scolding, stealing, fighting; laughing at the beautiful and splendid crash of walls and falling roofs.*

Above: The Great Chicago Fire not only destroyed the downtown section of the city, including city offices, the courthouse, stores, hotels and theatres, but it also wiped out the vice districts that had sprung up before the Civil War. *Courtesy of* Harper's Weekly.

Right: Rumors that Chicagoans were hanging looters were widespread but mostly untrue. Several shootings did take place, but there is no record of any criminals being hanged after the fire. General Philip Sheridan stated after the fire, "The people of the city are calm, quiet and well-disposed." *Courtesy of the Chicago Public Library*.

Soon after midnight, with the courthouse on fire, 350 prisoners were released from the jail in the basement. They immediately broke into a jewelry store and looted it.

The authorities were powerless to stop the looting during the fire, but they managed to stop it once the flames had burned themselves out. Within days, the city was being patrolled by two thousand special policemen, four hundred men of the regular force, six companies of the Illinois militia and four companies of troops from the regular army, commanded by General Philip Sheridan, who kept Chicago under martial law until October 22. Bizarre cases of arson, which seemed to follow every large conflagration, were discovered. Seven men who were caught setting fires were shot, and an eighth was beaten to death by a group of angry Chicagoans at Fourteenth Street and Fourth Avenue. His body was left lying in the street for twenty-four hours as a warning to others who might be inclined to start another blaze.

On the morning of October 10, 1871, W.D. Kerfoot, a well-known real estate agent, went to the ruins of his office on Washington Street, between Clark and Dearborn. With the assistance of his clerk and the clerk's

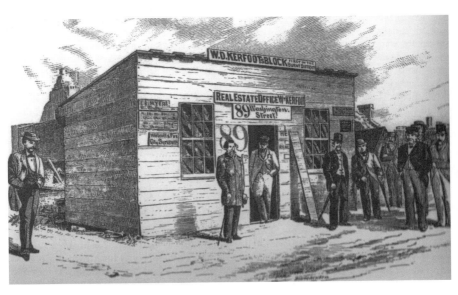

The first new building constructed in Chicago after the fire was erected by W.D. Kerfoot, a real estate agent. He cleared away the still smoldering ashes and constructed a wooden shanty where his office once stood. On the front of it, he placed a sign that read, "Kerfoot's Block—W.D. Kerfoot—Everything Gone but Wife, Children and Energy." The phrase became one of the most quoted in Chicago history. *Courtesy of* Harper's Weekly.

father, he cleared away the still smoldering ashes and hastily constructed a wooden shanty where his office once stood. In front of it, he placed a sign that read, "Kerfoot's Block—W.D. Kerfoot—Everything Gone but Wife, Children and Energy."

This was the first building erected in Chicago after the fire. By October 18, just ten days after the start of the disaster, business was being carried on in more than five thousand temporary structures, and within a year, more than ten thousand permanent structures had been erected. By the end of the decade, Chicago was a bigger and grander city than it had ever dreamed of being.

And no part of Chicago was rebuilt more quickly than the saloons, brothels, gambling houses and other resorts and habitats of the underworld. In less than a year after the fire, conditions were even worse than during the Civil War, with well over two thousand saloon licenses having been granted. As John J. Flinn wrote:

> *Concert halls, dives and brothels flourished. Every train load of strangers contained a large percentage of disreputable characters. Gamblers, bunko-steerers, confidence men, sharpers, and criminals of every description arrived in shoals to prey upon the disorganized and almost defenseless city; and the Police Department, hurriedly and inefficiently reorganized and scarcely large enough to patrol the burned district and protect new and unfinished buildings from vandals and looters, could do nothing to stop them. Again no man's life and property were safe, and citizens who ventured out at night were almost certain to be robbed, while the newspapers were filled with accounts of crimes and editorials demanding the arrest and punishment of criminals. The* Times *printed a list of Chicago's homicides in seven years and cried: "Nearly a hundred murders since 1865 and not a single neck stretched!"*

Chicago was poised to enter its true heyday of crime, and the heart of criminal activity could be found in the seedy and dangerous vice districts of the city.

BLOODY MAXWELL

As the thieves and criminals poured into Chicago, many of them found refuges from which to terrorize the city in two districts—the thirty-eighth police precinct and the twenty-second precinct. The thirty-eighth was located south of Division Street and northeast of the Chicago River. It boasted over four hundred saloons within its borders, and the worst of these were in a section known as "Little Hell," a network of brothels, dive hotels and concert saloons between LaSalle Street and the river.

One of the hotels in Little Hell catered exclusively to homosexuals, a novel concept at the time, and another was patronized only by dope addicts. Cocaine and morphine were sold openly there, right across the desk. In virtually every resort, knives and pistols could be rented by the hour, and men could be found who were willing to commit just about any crime for a handful of pocket change.

But the thirty-eighth precinct, despite the bloodshed carried out in Little Hell, was nothing compared to the twenty-second, which was better known as the "Bloody Maxwell" Street district. About two miles long and one mile wide, Bloody Maxwell was bounded on the north by Harrison Street, on the west by Wood Street, on the south by Sixteenth Street and on the east by the south branch of the Chicago River. It was known to have more saloons than any other district in the city.

The Maxwell Street Police Station had been constructed in 1889 to replace the old Second Precinct station, which was located in the heart of the "Terror District" and was abandoned that same year. This new building cost more than $50,000 to build. It was constructed of red and gray stone and was meant to be a refuge in the "wickedest police district to be found within the confines of civilization."

Captain William Ward, who had commanded the column of police officers blown up by the Haymarket Square bomb in 1886, was placed in command of Maxwell Street that first year. It was because of the unrest at Haymarket Square that the police force had greatly expanded its numbers and built two new stations, including the one at Maxwell Street. The station was meant to serve as a threat to worker unrest and also as a buffer between the central business district and the heavily populated immigrant areas that encroached on the business district from the south and west.

At that time, thousands of Jews, Italians, Greeks, Poles, Irish, Germans and other refugees from Europe were coming to the frenzied neighborhoods along Roosevelt Road, Taylor Street and Halsted. This was during the great wave of immigration that occurred between 1880 and 1920, and with the new arrivals came poverty, violence and crime. The *Chicago Tribune* said that all around the neighborhood "are corners, saloons and houses that have seen the rise, the operations, and even the deaths of some of the worst criminals the land has ever known."

Two blocks away from the station was the corner of Sangamon Street and Fourteenth Place, which was known by the notorious nickname of "Dead Man's Corner." Many of the murders there were connected to the Black Hand in Chicago, one of the city's first—and most mysterious—examples of organized crime.

The Black Hand was basically an extortion racket that looked for prosperous Italian immigrants who could be threatened. Such a man would receive a letter bearing the signature of the Black Hand, demanding a large amount of money. If the letter was ignored, or the man refused the demand, the windows of his home or business might be broken or his establishment bombed. If he continued to ignore the threat, he was liable to be killed. Most of the letters were crude and simply demanded cash. Others were courteously written, but no matter how they arrived, each brought a promise of death.

Literally hundreds of murders followed the arrival of Black Hand letters between 1900 and 1920. Despite what seemed to be an organized operation, the police could never uncover an operation that reached national, or even citywide, proportions. It was eventually realized that the Black Hand was not an actual gang but a method of crime.

Over the course of the first two decades of the twentieth century, there were an alleged four hundred murders in Chicago that were connected to the Black Hand. One hired killer used by the various gangs was known as the "Shotgun Man." He was believed to have been responsible for more than ten murders between January 1910 and March 1911. His identity was never discovered.

As the police attempted to investigate the actions of the Black Hand rackets, they made little progress. They made hundreds of arrests, but suspects were usually quickly released because no concrete evidence could be found against them. The few extortionists who were brought to trial were rarely prosecuted because witnesses and family members of the victim were threatened with death if they testified in court. Judges, jurors, members of the prosecutor's staff and even their families received threats.

The Black Hand gangs remained a frightening threat to Chicago's Italian community until about 1920, when a federal law forced them out of existence. Once the government started prosecuting the extortion demands as the misuse of the United States mail, dozens of gangsters were convicted, fined and sent to federal prisons. Unable to depend on corrupt local politicians to help them out, they had no chance to escape from prosecution. The prosecution of the crimes on a federal level brought an end to the extortion, bombings and murders, and the Black Hand faded away. Most of the gangsters found a new use for their skills with the coming of Prohibition.

While the Black Hand was certainly feared by the immigrant population of the Bloody Maxwell district, there were plenty of other crimes taking place, as well.

The area that earned the nickname Bloody Maxwell swarmed with hoodlums, burglars, killers and thieves, and they began finding a home there as early as the 1850s. It continued to be a breeding ground for criminals for three-quarters of a century, only enjoying a brief period of quiet during the 1880s, when the police, under Captain Simon O'Donnell, reduced the district "to a condition bordering upon respectability" by literally beating the underworld into submission. O'Donnell was later transferred out, however, and Bloody Maxwell relapsed into its previous state of depravity.

At the southern end of the Maxwell Street district was the Walsh School, a public institution and the scene of one of the bloodiest feuds in American history—a war between rival gangs of schoolboys that started in 1881 and continued for almost thirty years. During this time, several were killed and numerous others were shot, stabbed and beaten. The gangs called themselves the "Irishers" and the "Bohemians." The allegiance was not determined, as one might think, by nationality but rather by place of residence. The Irishers lived east of Johnson Street, and those who lived west of Johnson were the

Bohemians. For years, the boys carried knives and revolvers to school and occasionally slashed one another, or shot it out, in the classrooms, in the streets and on the playground. The last of the gun battles was fought in December 1905, when some twenty-five Irishers, led by Mike and George McGinnis, marched against an almost equal number of Bohemians, commanded by Joe Fischer. Between forty and fifty shots were fired before the police arrived, but no one was hit. The ages of the gangsters ranged from ten to fifteen years old, and many of the boys were so small that they had to use both hands to raise their revolvers to fire them. For many years after this last climactic battle, every boy who attended Walsh School had to be searched before he was allowed to enter.

As the neighborhood turned from mostly Irish to a collection of immigrants from various countries, many of the Irish formed gangs to combat what they saw as a German and Jewish invasion during the 1870s and 1880s. The German and Jewish hoodlums organized in self-defense, as did other nationalities. For several years, the racial and national lines were strictly drawn, but in time, origins made little difference. Soon, there were many gangs with members from a half dozen different countries.

There were a number of dangerous and dominant gangs in the Maxwell Street district during the late 1800s. One of them was the Johnson Street gang, which was led by Buff Higgins. Another was the Henry Street gang, under the leadership of Chris Merry, who once fought a two-hour shootout with police and was eventually hanged for kicking his invalid wife to death. The Mortell-McGraw gang was commanded by Bill Mortell, who spent many years in prison, and Jack McGraw, who later reformed and led a peaceful life as a bricklayer. The McGanns were led by one-legged felon Jimmy McGann and his five sons. The family was a group of successful thieves for many years, but their wicked ways eventually caught up with them. By 1903, one of the sons was in a reformatory, another in state prison, another in the Cook County jail and another was dead, killed by his own father during a drunken brawl.

Of equal importance with these rough gangs, though in a different category, was a band of thieves known as the Weiss gang, or White gang, formed in 1866 when the six sons and two daughters of widow Margaret Weiss of Maxwell Street married into the Renich family of ten daughters and two sons. The children of these unions also intermarried, and by the late 1890s, along with cousins and other relatives, the inbred tribe numbered more than one hundred people, all of whom were said by the police to be criminals. About twenty of them ended up in prison.

Bloody Maxwell

For many years, the headquarters of the gang was an isolated house on Cooper Street in Lakeview, where they often stored wagonloads of stolen property. The leaders of the outfit were George and Mary Miller, but the real brains behind everything was Mrs. Renich's sister, Eva Gussler, who was better known as "Eva the Cow." She was an expert pickpocket and one of the best shoplifters to ever operate in Chicago. Eva planned and directed the gang's nefarious enterprises and also took charge of the children, teaching them to steal almost as soon as they were able to walk. One of their most clever methods of shoplifting involved having a woman wear a large skirt, under which would be a small child. As the woman walked slowly about the store, the little girl walked along under her skirts. When the woman saw something she wanted to steal, she "accidentally" knocked it off the counter and onto the floor. The child then picked it up and stuffed it into a pocket that had been sewn inside the skirt.

Buff Higgins, leader of the Johnson Street gang, was a typical product of Bloody Maxwell. He carried two guns with him at all times and never did an honest day's work in his life, or so some of the old-timers used to say. He lived on the proceeds of burglaries, gang thefts and holdups, and when not occupied in crime, he loafed about in the saloons and brothels of the district.

Higgins was born in Ireland in 1871 and came to America with his family when he was only two years old. In 1874, his family moved to Chicago and settled on Johnson Street in the Maxwell district. Buff attended the Walsh School for several years, and in the 1880s, he was one of the captains of the Irishers. He quit school when he was thirteen years old and organized a boys' gang that broke windows, robbed fruit stands and harassed the local merchants. By the time he was fifteen, Higgins was an accomplished thief and a regular fixture in the saloons and whorehouses. By eighteen, he had formed the formidable Johnson Street gang. He ruled his corner of the district for more than five years, committing countless thefts and holdups, killing at least two men and wounding many others, including two or three police officers. He was arrested many times, but the merchants and others he had robbed refused to testify against him for fear of reprisals by his men.

Higgins was never in serious trouble until the early morning of September 3, 1893, when he broke into the home of Peter McCooey on Johnson Street. He was accompanied by two of his men, Red Gary and Johnny Mortell, a "notorious character" who was sentenced to life in prison in 1880 for killing a policeman but was paroled within two years.

The three men entered McCooey's bedroom after filling a bag with loot from other parts of the house. Higgins was going through the pockets of a pair of trousers when McCooey suddenly woke up and jumped out of bed. Higgins quickly shot him. McCooey, who recognized Higgins, lived long enough to name his murderer, and the burglars were arrested after a desperate fight with the police. Gary and Mortell were sent to prison, and Higgins was convicted of murder in the first degree. He was hanged at the Cook County jail on March 23, 1894.

Chris Merry, who ran the Henry Street gang, was described by the *Chicago Tribune* as "one of the worst criminals that ever lived in Chicago." And while his criminal record was certainly surpassed by many, it is doubtful that Bloody Maxwell or any other section of the city ever produced a more fierce and bloody fighter. He was remarkably well suited for bare-knuckle brawling, and few men possessed the courage to withstand the heavy blows of this bull-necked figure, with his enormously long arms, huge hands and brutal, pig-like face. Merry was sullen and remorseful by habit, but he was subject to terrible fits of rage, brought about by little or no provocation. During those times, he was described as being like a "demon unleashed, and acted more like a mad animal than like a human being." While fighting, Merry continually barked and grunted and fought with his fists, teeth, feet and any other weapon he could get his hands on. He had disfigured many of the men who dared to stand up to him. The police generally left him alone, but at the times when it was necessary to bring him in, six or eight officers were generally sent to arrest him.

Merry claimed to be a peddler, but the wagon he drove about Bloody Maxwell was nothing more than a means of flight and a carrier of stolen goods. Emboldened by the widespread fear generated by Chris Merry, the Henry Street gang became one of the most successful theft rings in the district. Merry and his men sometimes drove along Maxwell and Halsted Streets in broad daylight, boldly taking what they wanted from stores and outside stands. There were few who were brave enough to stop him. Those who tried to stand against him never managed to do it more than once.

The Johnson Street, Henry Street and Mortell-McGraw gangs vanished after the deaths or imprisonments of their leaders, but many other gangs continued to make Bloody Maxwell as much of a terror district as it had been under the rule of Buff Higgins or Chris Merry. One of the most feared of these was the Daly gang, which was headquartered on Maxwell Street and broke up in 1905 when the police arrested Tom and Jack Daly and sent them to Joliet Penitentiary. The Forty-twos of Taylor Street was another dangerous outfit. It had started as a harmless neighborhood play group and eventually turned into a notorious band of pickpockets, car thieves and vandals.

The Valley gang of Fifteenth Street organized in the mid-1890s and remained in existence for nearly forty years. The first important leaders of the outfit were "Big Heinie" Miller and Jimmy Farley, skilled pickpockets and burglars who ran things in the early 1900s. They were both locked up at Joliet in 1905, together with two other members of the gang, "Tootsie" Bill Hughes and "Cooney the Fox," whom police officers of the time called "the smoothest thieves who ever worked the Maxwell Street district."

After the arrest of Miller and Farley, the gang was led by Red Bolton for several years. He also ended his career in state prison, serving a life sentence for murder. Bolton was followed by Paddy Ryan, also known as "Paddy the Bear." This red-faced, obese monster was only a little over five feet tall and weighed more than 250 pounds. He ran a run-down saloon on South Halsted Street and was one of the most feared men in the history of Bloody Maxwell. Ryan was murdered in 1920 by Walter Quinlan, who had taken the wife of an imprisoned gangster and was badly beaten for this breach of underworld etiquette. After serving a few years in prison for Ryan's murder, Quinlan opened a saloon at Seventeenth and Loomis Streets, which became a hangout for local gunmen. During one raid on the saloon, police confiscated a dozen automatic pistols, ten bulletproof vests and two machine guns. Quinlan was finally killed by Paddy Ryan's son, who was known as "Paddy the Fox."

The most successful leaders of the Valley gang were Terry Druggan and Frankie Lake, who gained their greatest infamy as beer providers during the Prohibition era. Under their leadership, the gang concentrated its efforts on bootlegging and eventually controlled a string of breweries. Druggan and Lake made millions, and even the men who loaded their trucks, they often boasted, "wore silk shirts and rode in Rolls-Royce automobiles."

In 1924, after refusing to answer questions that had been put to them by Judge James Wilkerson of the United States District Court, Druggan and Lake were sentenced to a year in prison on contempt charges. Several months later, a newspaper reporter called at the county jail to see them and was told that the two men were not available. "They had an appointment downtown and will be back after dinner," he was told. After an investigation, the confused reporter learned that both Druggan and Lake, in return for $20,000 in bribes, had been given extraordinary privileges. While supposedly incarcerated and treated like other prisoners, they actually spent more time in downtown restaurants and in their own apartments than they did in jail.

They were permitted to come and go as they pleased, and the death cell at the jail had been turned into a private office where the gangsters received as many visitors as they liked and even issued orders for criminal activities. As a result of this arrangement being exposed, Sheriff Peter Hoffman and Jailer Wesley Westbrook were jailed for three months in contempt of court.

Just north of the Maxwell Street Police Station was the liquor warehouse of the six "Terrible" Genna brothers, Angelo, Pete, Tony, Jim, Sam and Mike. On the eve of Prohibition, they had been granted a special dispensation from the government to sell industrial alcohol from this location on Taylor Street. The formula for the brew had been invented by their brother-in-law Harry Spignola, and the Gennas paid neighborhood residents fifteen dollars a week to cook up a home-brew, which contained rotgut whiskey with caramel or coal tar added for color. The result was so vile that it actually killed the warehouse rats that were curious enough to sample it. From the filthy warehouse, the Gennas paid off the cops of the district to leave them alone after it became apparent that the alcohol was not for "industrial" purposes. The Gennas sold the mixture for three dollars a barrel, which was half the going rate that was being charged by Irish bootlegger Dion O'Banion, who hated the Gennas. Eventually, their mutual dislike bubbled over into violence, and war erupted. The Gennas were all but wiped out in a few short years, and the warehouse was closed down in 1926.

Bloody Maxwell was one of the most prolific of Chicago's crime-breeding areas, but it was only one out of many. Criminal gangs developed in and dominated every vice district in the city. The *Chicago Tribune* wrote:

> *Chicago is gang-ridden to such extremes that the safety of life, property and happiness are only proverbs, and, like many proverbs, absolutely untrue, and the real facts are that life, property and happiness are only safe when they are protected by locality, strength of arm, or firearms. Chicago is infested with a gang of hoodlums to whom the law is a thing to mock at and by whom the revolver and the bullet and the strong arm of the officer are the only things that are feared, and who, after dark in every locality, and through the day time in many localities, menace the decent citizen's life and belongings at every step. Chicago is terrorized by criminals who have helped make the name "Chicago" a byword for crime-breeding throughout the country.*

CUSTOM HOUSE PLACE

During the late 1800s, the Custom House Place vice district became one of the most renowned red-light districts in America, offering not only the vilest of Chicago's dens of iniquity but also some of its most elegant parlor houses.

During the Civil War, there had been perhaps eight or nine brothels in the northern part of this district, but after the Great Fire, this portion of the area was mostly taken over by businesses, and the vice moved south of Harrison Street. Custom House Place sprang from the ashes of the Great Fire and soon earned its sordid reputation. For nearly thirty years, the area was regarded as a blight on the downtown. Like most segregated vice areas, where gambling, liquor and prostitution were indulged, the Custom House thrived on not only its proximity to the railroads but also an alliance with the police. The closest police could be found at the nearby armory station, and they turned a blind eye to questionable activity in the district—for a price, of course.

The Custom House district existed between Harrison Street to the north and Polk Street and the Dearborn train station to the south. It is an area more popularly known as "Printer's Row" today. The boundaries of the area tended to change and expand with the opening of each new saloon or house of ill repute. It also tended to shrink when any of the owners neglected to make their protection payments. A police raid usually followed such absent-minded behavior.

The Dearborn Station became essential to operations in the area as it made a perfect recruiting spot for prostitutes during the gaslight era. Naïve young women who stepped off the train were often greeted by one of the army of pimps who waited in the station. From that point, they were introduced to immoral acts and lured into the "scarlet patch" of the Custom House district.

Detective Clifton Woolridge described Custom House Place in 1893, when the district was at the height of its fame during the World's Columbian Exposition in Chicago:

Here at all hours of the day and night women could be seen at doors and windows, frequently half-clad, making an exhibition of themselves and using vulgar and obscene language. At almost all of these places there were sliding windows, or windows that hung on hinges and swung aside. These windows were used by the women to invite pedestrians on the street to enter these places and also for the purpose of exhibiting themselves.

All of the houses were equipped with electric bells, and a sentinel whose duty it was to watch for the police and give a signal to the inmates, was stationed at each end of the street between Polk and Harrison…It was no unusual thing in those days to see from fifty to one hundred women lounging in the doors and windows of this block at one time. The habitués of this place embraced every nationality, both black and white, their ages ranging from eighteen to fifty years. The costumes worn by these people embraced every kind known to the human race. Some were in tights, some having nothing on but a loose Mother Hubbard, made of some flashy material which resembled a mosquito bar, through which the entire form of the woman could be seen. Others were dressed as jockeys, while others had no sleeves on their dresses. Their waist was cut so low that their bosoms were entirely exposed, and some were dressed almost exclusively in the garb which nature gave them when they were born.

In these houses could be found every low and demoralizing phase of life that the human mind could think of. Many of these women were even lower than brutes.

Exorbitant rents were charged for these buildings, some of them bringing as high as $250 to $275 per month. Several enterprising landladies rented and furnished from one to four houses each and sublet them for $15 to $25 per day in advance. Among the worst characters on the street was Mary Hastings, who rented and furnished four of these places and received as high as $25 per day for each of them…In order to pay these exorbitant prices these women were compelled to commit crimes, and nearly every man who entered one of them was robbed before he got out.

Custom House Place

The activities of the prostitutes in Custom House Place became so obnoxious that in 1896 a committee from the Civic Federation called on Mayor George B. Swift and demanded that he enforce the laws that existed against the maintaining of brothels. The committee argued that the whores were a menace to society, that their orgies could be seen by those who passed the windows of the disorderly houses and that they were leading astray many young boys who came to the district out of curiosity.

Accompanied by Chief of Police J.J. Badenoch, Mayor Swift toured Custom House Place and was profoundly shocked and disturbed by what he saw there—but he didn't do anything to close the houses down. Instead, he ordered the owners to paint their windows and keep them closed so that no one could see inside.

Of all of the brothels in the red-light districts, the ones that gave the police the most trouble were the "panel houses," which were more robbers' dens than brothels. Often an unsophisticated visitor would stumble into one of these places, where he might be drugged and tied up while an accomplice slipped through a hidden panel in the wall and liberated him of his valuables. More often, the secret panels hid thieves with long hooks who could lift a customer's wallet from pants hanging on the bedpost, placed there while he was otherwise engaged. Few of these victims would report the robbery to the police, lest they suffer the humiliation of having their names printed in the newspaper.

This method of robbery was said to have been pioneered by a notorious New York thief and brothel madam named Moll Hodges, who also operated panel houses in Philadelphia. The first resort to try it in Chicago was opened at Clark and Adams Streets about 1865 by Lizzie Clifford, who had worked for Hodges in New York. The brothel was destroyed in the Great Fire, and Chicago was relatively free of such places until the 1880s, when they began reappearing in large numbers. By the 1890s, there were likely about two hundred of them in the city, mostly in Custom House Place, Clark and State Streets and Plymouth Place. As much as $10,000 was reported at the Harrison Street police station as having been taken from panel houses in a single night—the officers often logged from fifty to one hundred complaints. One can only wonder how many robberies were never reported at all.

In 1896, the police managed to shut down fifty-two panel houses and closed about forty-five more in 1898. During that same year, the keepers of twenty-eight of these places were arrested, and while there is no record to say that any of them were ever punished, by centering the attack on such establishments, the police soon put an end to the business.

Chicago detective Clifton R. Woolridge referred to himself as the "World's Greatest Detective, the Incorruptible Sherlock Holmes of America." He was instrumental in closing down the panel houses in the Custom House Place district and made hundreds of arrests in the city's vice districts.

The man most responsible for the all-out attack on panel houses was Detective Clifton Woolridge, a scourge of the Chicago underworld in the late 1800s and early 1900s and one of the most unusual police officers to ever work in the Windy City. Woolridge was often thought of as a comic figure to other officers, especially after he arrested a girl for smoking a cigarette on the street or when he was dressed in one of the seventy-five disguises that he kept in the squad room of the Harrison Street police station. He loved to brag and referred to himself as the "World's Greatest Detective, the Incorruptible Sherlock Holmes of America." He wrote in his books that "no braver, more honest or efficient police officer ever wore a star or carried a club." In spite of this, he really was an excellent policeman and undoubtedly caused more problems for the red-light districts than any other policeman in Chicago.

Woolridge served the Chicago police department from 1888 to 1910 and in that time made nearly twenty thousand arrests, sent two hundred lawbreakers to the penitentiary and three thousand to the House of Corrections, rescued one hundred girls from brothels and white slavery, recovered more than $100,000 in stolen property, refused hundreds of bribes and was shot at forty-four times and wounded more than twenty times. He was a small man, not more than five feet, six inches tall and weighing just over 150 pounds, but he was a fierce fighter, and many larger hoodlums were terrified of him. He always carried two guns, and while he never killed a man in the line of duty, he wounded scores of criminals who dared to cross him.

Custom House Place

During the early 1890s—with only slight assistance from the rest of the Chicago Police Department, if you believe Woolridge's version of events—the detective broke up one of the most devious criminal gangs to ever operate in the city. They were a group of female African American thieves who prowled the vice districts of the South Side and committed hundreds of holdups before they were all finally sent to prison. They usually worked in pairs and were armed with revolvers, razors, brass knuckles, knives and baseball bats. Among these female hoodlums were Emma Ford and her sister; Pearl Smith; Flossie Moore; Hattie Washington; Laura Johnson; Mary White, who was also known as "the Strangler"; and Ella Sherwood, an opium addict who was known for her violent temper. In 1893, Ella Sherwood gave a saloonkeeper $375, the proceeds of a robbery, to keep for her until things quieted down after the theft. When he refused to give her back the money, she broke all of his windows with a baseball bat and then stood in the doorway of his place and emptied two revolvers into the mirror and bottles behind the bar.

For several years, this unusual gang was headquartered in Custom House Place, in one of the panel houses kept by Lizzie Davenport, perhaps the most successful thief of this class in Chicago. According to the police, more than $500,000 was stolen in Lizzie's resorts over a ten-year period. It was not out of the ordinary for from ten to fifteen robberies to occur in her Custom House Place brothels in one night. To protect her thieving whores from the authorities, Lizzie built a closet of three-inch oak planks, with a heavy door, where they could be hidden in case of a raid. Woolridge managed to drive them out of their hiding place by drilling holes in the door and blowing pepper into the closet.

According to records, and Detective Woolridge, the most dangerous of the strong-arm women were Emma Ford and Flossie Moore. Both women were expert pickpockets, as well as stickup artists and panel workers. Emma Ford stood just over six feet tall, weighed two hundred pounds and had arms so long that she could "scratch her kneecaps without stooping." She was a dangerous fighter and would never submit to arrest, unless it was at the point of a revolver. She was dreaded by police officers since it took two of them to handle her and hated by the wardens and guards of the various prisons where she served short sentences. Once, in the Cook County jail, she nearly drowned a guard by holding him under the water in a horse trough. At the House of Correction, she went on a rampage in the laundry and horribly disfigured several other female inmates with a hot flatiron. After each term in prison, Ford continued her criminal career, and as late as 1903, she was still considered the terror of the red-light districts.

Flossie Moore was once described as the "most notorious female bandit and footpad that ever operated in Chicago." She was also one of the most successful, working the vice districts from 1888 to the late spring of 1893. In that time, she stole more than $125,000. She always carried a large roll of bills in the bosom of her dress and another in her stocking. She kept a lawyer on a $125-per-month retainer and appeared at balls given by Negro prostitutes and brothel keepers in gowns that cost over $500 each. She gave her lover, a white man named "Handsome" Harry Gray, an allowance of $25 per day. She was arrested and released on bail as often as ten times in a single day, and in one year, she was held for trial in the criminal courts thirty-six times. She paid over $10,000 in fines to the Harrison Street police station, and once when she was fined $100, she laughed at the judge and told him, "Make it $200, I got money to burn!"

Despite the number of times she was arrested, Moore managed to escape punishment until March 1893, when she was sent to Joliet prison for stealing forty-three dollars from an elderly farmer. Prison officials said that she was one of the most deranged women ever confined at Joliet. She twice tried to kill the matron and spent six months of her sentence in solitary confinement. She returned to Chicago after her sentence was up but left the city and went east. She was last heard from in New York in 1900. After that, she vanished from the pages of history.

In addition to the panel houses, there were also scores of standard brothels in Custom House Place—along with dives, ratholes and terrifying places that only the most desperate man would frequent. One of the worst characters in Custom House Place, briefly mentioned earlier by Detective Woolridge, was Mary Hastings.

Mary came to Chicago in 1888, and in her mid-twenties, she already had a long experience with brothels. She had worked in and operated sporting houses in Brussels, where she was born, and in Paris, Toronto, Denver, Portland and San Francisco, where she had served a six-month prison sentence for practices that offended even the denizens of the notorious Barbary Coast. In Chicago, she established a whorehouse at 144 Custom House Place, about halfway between Polk and Harrison Streets, and also operated a saloon a few doors away. The saloon was run by her lover, Tom Gaynor, who eventually defrauded her out of both money and property. In 1892, she furnished and sublet the four dives referred to by Detective Woolridge and that same year built another sporting house on South Dearborn Street, near Twenty-second.

A vintage illustration of infamous madam Mary Hastings and one of her brothels. She operated a number of resorts in Custom House Place until finally being arrested and put out of business in 1897.

For several years, she avoided trouble with the law by paying the local beat cops two dollars each week and providing them with free meals, drinks and girls whenever they wanted them. She also made, as was the custom of the time, regular payments to ward politicians and to the inspectors and captains at the Harrison Street police station.

Mary supervised the operation of all her properties but made number 144 her actual residence. She gave the establishment, which was a small house that only offered about twelve girls, her close personal attention. It was a particularly vicious place, and Mary often boasted that all of the girls had been thrown out of "decent houses" for stealing and fighting. If a girl was good enough to get into one of the first-class parlor houses, then she was too good for Mary Hastings. She also bragged that no man could imagine an act of perversion that her whores would not perform— and proved it on "circus nights," which were held two or three times each month.

From the start of her career in Chicago, Mary occasionally bought girls from procurers and sometimes financed the activities of these traffickers in white slaves. Early in 1893, she entered the business herself on a large scale, making trips to other cities and returning with young girls who ranged in age from thirteen to seventeen. She had induced them to accompany her to Chicago by promising them legitimate employment. Most of the girls were taken to one of her brothels in Custom House Place, where they were locked in a room and their clothing was taken away. After that, they were broken into what those in the red-light districts called "the life," a process that involved rape and assorted brutal treatment. Girls who were procured in this manner were used to fill vacancies in Mary's resorts or were sold to other madams, ranging in price from $50 to $300, depending on their age and beauty.

The police, who would not take procuring seriously until a few years later when publicity forced them to take action, knew of Mary Hastings's activities, but were unable to obtain conclusive evidence against her until the fall of 1895, when she brought nine girls into Chicago from Cleveland. Four of the victims managed to escape from a brothel by tying bedsheets together and climbing out of a window. Three of them made their way to the Harrison Street police station, but the fourth disappeared and was never seen again. The other five girls were rescued by a raiding party of police detectives.

Two indictments were returned against Mary Hastings, and she was released on bail provided by Tom Gaynor. She immediately fled to Canada, and when her case came to trial, her bail was forfeited. She eventually returned to Chicago, although she managed to stay out of the courts until the summer of 1897, by which time the witnesses had vanished, and the state was forced to abandon the prosecution. Meanwhile, Mary had assigned all of her property to Gaynor in her absence, and when she attempted to take back over the running of her brothels, he threw her out. He finally gave her $200, and she left for Toledo, never to return to Chicago again.

But not all of the brothels on Custom House Place were seedy and dangerous. The most infamous bordello in the district was Carrie Watson's place on South Clark Street. Despite the area in which it was located, the beautiful Miss Watson's "house" enjoyed a wide reputation for being a charming place, with Carrie having sixty women in her employ. Over the years, she has become a character of legend in the annals of Chicago vice, and her beginnings in the city have long been the subject of fascination.

Caroline Victoria Watson was the daughter of an upper-middle-class family in Buffalo, New York, where she was born in 1850. According to the lore, she grew up and saw her older sisters and their friends doing little more than eking out a living working in stores or slaving away as domestic help. Knowing that such a life was not for her, Carrie was said to have taken stock of her capabilities and decided that her greatest opportunity lay in the field of prostitution. So, in 1866, sixteen and still a virgin, she came to Chicago and became an inmate of a brothel called the Mansion in order to learn the business and to prepare herself for her future career as a madam. She remained in the house for two years, hoarding her money and learning the ways of the customers.

When a madam named Annie Stewart left Chicago in 1868 after killing a police officer, Carrie Watson took over the lease of her bordello on South Clark Street, between Polk and Taylor. She immediately installed new beds and furnishings and hired new girls. She later bought the building with the help of her security man, Al Smith, who ran a saloon and gambling house up the street. Annie Stewart had run her brothel as a wide-open operation, admitting any customer who came calling, but from the beginning, Carrie catered exclusively to the carriage trade and was just beginning to build up a wealthy clientele when the Great Fire disrupted businesses of every type. According to legend, the fire destroyed the house, but in fact, the property was almost two blocks south of the burned area and was not damaged. The fire hurt her business badly, though, and it took nearly two years for Carrie to recover.

Early in 1873, Carrie made extensive alterations to the property, and when they were completed, she reopened what must have been the finest resort of its kind in America. The three-story brownstone mansion had five parlors, more than twenty bedrooms, a billiard room and, reportedly, a bowling alley in the basement. The furniture was expensively upholstered, imported rugs covered the floors and the walls were hung with rare artwork and European tapestries. A three-piece orchestra played music, and wine was brought into the parlors in silver buckets and served in gold goblets for ten dollars per bottle. The girls, who numbered ten to twenty ordinarily but twice that number during the World's Fair, received callers in silk gowns and performed on linen sheets. The business of the house was conducted with great subtlety, and there was no red light over the door, no red curtains and no hawkers hustling men in off the street. The only advertising at the resort, so the story goes, was done by a parrot, trained to say, "Carrie Watson. Come in, gentlemen." The parrot spent the daylight hours in a cage just outside the front door.

Carrie's brothel operated for nearly twenty-five years and enjoyed worldwide fame, thanks to its high prices, the loveliness of the ladies who worked there and the luxurious surroundings of the building. Carrie Watson herself, who was extremely rich by the time she retired, was renowned for her silks and diamonds, her two white carriages with bright yellow wheels, her charities and the fact that she paid a larger personal property tax than most Chicago millionaires. Shang Andrews's *Sporting Life* stated with enthusiasm that "in all the world, there is not another Carrie Watson!"

By the time of the Columbian Exposition in 1893, Chicago had become known as the "Paris of America" for its many illicit attractions. Reformist W.T. Stead, in his book *If Christ Came to Chicago*, counted thirty-seven bordellos, forty-six saloons, eleven pawnbrokers, an opium den and numerous gambling parlors in the Custom House Place district while writing his exposé on Chicago vice.

The official stance on such districts was to leave them alone, as long as the operators, thieves and undesirables stayed in the district and kept to themselves. However, this was rarely the case. Granted a wide berth by city officers, the dealers in vice exploited the situation, with prostitutes being arrested in the theatre district and posing as salesgirls in reputable stores. By 1903, conditions had become intolerable, and reformers would no longer stand for it. A wave of criminal indictments, pushed through by church groups and the mayor himself, sent the vice operators reeling. Most of the operators in the district moved to the South Side Levee, where they were welcomed with open arms. Custom House Place had vanished completely by 1910.

Custom House Place

After that, the deserted area was slowly taken over by commercial printing houses and bookbinderies, creating the name the district bears today: Printer's Row. Eventually, the printing houses joined the bordellos, and they, too, faded away. About 1979, the area was converted into the condominium and rental community that exists today. The railroad freight yards have also disappeared, although Dearborn station remains. It has been converted into a small shopping mall serving the residents of this quiet street. The Custom House Place vice district is now only a memory.

CHICAGO'S WICKEDEST PEOPLE

Satan (impatiently) to Newcomer: The trouble with you Chicago people is, that you think you are the best people down here; whereas you are merely the most numerous.
—*Mark Twain, "Pudd'nhead Wilson's New Calendar," 1897*

Chicago is a place of unusual people and strange characters, but the vice districts of the late nineteenth and early twentieth centuries produced a larger than normal number of eccentric figures. Many of them have become Chicago legends, and in almost every case, the red-light districts of the Windy City could not have existed without them.

"BATHHOUSE" JOHN COUGHLIN AND "HINKY-DINK" KENNA

There is no city in America that has been as maligned as Chicago when it comes to politicians, corruption and questionable voting practices. Even Chicago's most famous nickname, the "Windy City," comes from the hot air that was expelled by the city's politicians rather than from the speed of local air currents.

This reputation dates back to the earliest days of the city, when blatant voter fraud managed to gain Chicago its charter. It is no wonder that "vote early and vote often" became a phrase to ridicule Chicago voting habits in years to come.

Since that time, the city has become known for its backroom politics, "smoke-filled" rooms, backhanded favors and outright bribes. Needless to say, Chicago's politicians have long been colorful characters, starting with those who served as mayor.

The mayors of the city were always men of importance. It is true that the early pioneer mayors are barely remembered today, but later on, as the mayors became more entrenched in the city's political system, they became capable of causing riots and firing the entire police force. Some of them were controlled by gamblers, befriended by gangsters or manipulated behind the scenes by merchants and businessmen. Occasionally, good men would be elected to office, and each would try valiantly to clean up the town. They would start reform movements to purge the city of corrupt officials, to close down saloons on Sunday and brothels on weeknights and to raid all of the gambling dens within spitting distance of city hall. But in most cases, these good men were not supported by an honest administration, and soon the people of Chicago would be drawn to another man, who spoke louder and made more promises than the rest. For the most part, it seems that the best Chicago mayors have been the ones who have more or less let the city run them rather than try to run the city. They have been men who have enforced the laws to the point that respectable citizens could walk the streets but never caused enough trouble to scare off the tourists or irritate the local folks who wanted to drink, gamble or carouse a little.

Some authors have said that Chicago is a religious town, but it is not religious in any traditional way. The town has a moral façade that it maintains to disguise its sinful activities. Chicago loves the money that its reputation for being a bloody city tied to gangsters and ghosts brings in, but the "official" stance on the subject rejects this image. Many of the city's mayors have epitomized this attitude. They made deals with crooks and gangsters while issuing self-righteous statements about how awful crime is.

However, it has been proven time and time again that you don't have to be the mayor to run Chicago. The story goes that a Chicago politician was once asked if there was ever a good, hardworking, honest alderman on the city council. According to the story, he admitted that there had once been, but they had given him a lesser job and made him a U.S. senator. The person who had asked the question was dumbfounded. A U.S. senator was less powerful than being a Chicago alderman? The politician shrugged. "Sure," he allegedly replied. "How many jobs does a senator control compared to an alderman?"

There were two Chicago aldermen most responsible for the continuation of vice in the city, "Bathhouse" John Coughlin and "Hinky-Dink" Kenna. Their domain was Chicago's South Side Levee District, which took shape during the Columbian Exposition in 1893, when thousands of people from all over the world descended on the city. Many believe that the growth of a vice district on the South Side may have been what spurred Potter Palmer to flee the region and to build his castle on North Lake Shore Drive, far from the illicit goings-on. He was not the only one of the wealthy to flee, either. Prairie Avenue soon fell into gradual ruin as the Levee began to grow and prosper in the early 1900s.

Visitors to the district could partake of just about every form of vice imaginable, from drink to women, and it became a seedbed of crime that would go on to spawn men like Al Capone, Johnny Torrio and the generations that followed them to become the modern Chicago Outfit. Three vice rings formed the criminal organization that ruled the Levee and provided the area's various forms of entertainment. The area was filled with brothels, gambling parlors and saloons of every type. While reformers considered the Levee District a "blight" on the city of Chicago, it brought in millions of dollars every year and was one of the wealthiest "business" districts in the city.

And while criminal elements ran the district, there was no question as to the identity of the real "bosses" of the Levee. Michael "Hinky-Dink" Kenna and "Bathhouse" John Coughlin ran the notorious, gangster-infested First Ward for almost four decades, between 1897 and 1938. They made a legendary team, collecting graft and doling out favors in the area to those who paid the most. In 1911, when Mayor Harrison gave the word to Captain Patrick J. Harding to order his divisional inspector John Wheeler to close down the famed Everleigh Club brothel, the inspector did nothing until he received the okay from aldermen Kenna and Coughlin.

Coughlin was known as "Bathhouse" because he had once been a masseur in a Turkish bath. He was a large, poetry-spouting buffoon who was known for being outgoing, goodhearted and a bizarre dresser, sporting garishly colored waistcoats. His poetry often appeared in Chicago newspapers, and after hearing some of his public statements, many mistook him for being simple-minded. Mayor Harrison once asked his partner,

Aldermen of Chicago's First Ward, "Hinky-Dink" Kenna and "Bathhouse" John Coughlin. *Courtesy of the Chicago Historical Society.*

Kenna, if Bathhouse was crazy or taken with drugs. Kenna replied that he was neither. "To tell you the God's truth, Mayor, they ain't found a name for it yet."

Kenna was Coughlin's mirror opposite. He was small, glum and quietly dressed and was known for being shrewd and close-mouthed. At Kenna's Workingman's Exchange on Clark Street, patrons were served what was referred to as the "Largest and Coolest Schooner of Beer in the City" and the best free lunch around, too. There were no orchestras here, no women, no music and no selling to minors. Here, for more than twenty years, the bums, the homeless and the jobless of the First Ward ate and drank for a nickel. Kenna also found jobs for the down and out and often rescued them from trouble with the police.

He also told them how to vote, and in more than forty years, he never lost an election or primary. He and Bathhouse created this astonishing record by marshaling the ward's party workers on election day to get votes from railroad hands, tramps, thieves and any other warm bodies available. They were taken to a polling place and given already marked ballots to be deposited in a box. When they returned with the unmarked ballots (taken from the polling place), they could turn them in for a fee of fifty cents or a dollar. Those ballots were then marked and used at another polling place, where the whole scheme was repeated.

The two men made an unlikely pair but were a highly effective and increasingly wealthy duo. In addition to the other services they offered, such as guaranteed voting in the First Ward, they also provided protection for a variety of illicit enterprises. They exacted regular and weekly tributes that ranged from $25 per week from the small brothels to as much as $100 from the larger ones. They received an additional fee if drinks were sold or gambling occurred there. They also offered fees for legal work, such as stopping indictments for charges of grand larceny, pandering, theft or kidnapping. These fees could range from $500 to $2,000.

They were able to provide such services thanks to the fact that Coughlin and Kenna had men who were beholden to them in every municipal, county, state and federal office in the city. They controlled the jobs of city workers, including inspectors and the police, and were also, as aldermen, in a position to grant favors to respectable businessmen in Chicago. They could usually count on a routine take of between $15,000 and $30,000 per year, over and above the stipend of $3 per council meeting that they received from the city. Special votes that were purchased brought them anywhere from $8,000 to $100,000 each, depending on the importance of the matter. The two men went carefully about their business, filling the requests that the financiers of Chicago were willing to pay for, such as zoning variances, permits, tax deductions, licenses and other amenities.

However, things didn't always go smoothly, and the pair did sometimes manage to attract attention, both personally and professionally. For instance, one of Bathhouse's pet projects was the construction of a zoo on land that he owned in Colorado Springs in 1902. The zoo featured a refugee elephant from the Lincoln Park Zoo that had managed to lose part of her trunk in a trapdoor. Princess Alice, as she was called, was purchased by Coughlin and shipped to Colorado, where she caught a severe cold in the winter of 1906.

Coughlin suggested that she be given whiskey, which cured his own ailments, and so keepers gave the elephant an entire quart, which quickly cured her cold. After that, Princess Alice acquired a serious taste for the hard stuff and began searching the zoo, looking for visitors with flasks. She would beg for drinks, and when whiskey was given to her, she would sip it daintily and then go off somewhere to pass out.

As mentioned, Bathhouse was also noted for his horrible poetry. Epics that he penned included titles like "She Sleeps by the Drainage Canal," "Ode to a Bathtub," "They're Tearing Up Clark Street Again," "Why Did They Build the Lovely Lake So Close to the Horrible Shore?" and others. It was later revealed that John Kelley, a reporter for the *Chicago Tribune*, was the actual author of many of Coughlin's poems, which he read regularly at city council meetings. But only Coughlin would have taken credit for a terrible song that he wrote called "Dear Midnight of Love," which was performed for the first and last time at the Auditorium Theatre in October 1899.

Bad poetry aside, it was not weak prose that brought Coughlin and Kenna to the attention of the public and every reform organization in Chicago from 1897 onward. It was constantly, and justifiably, assumed that the two of them were corrupt, although nothing was ever proven against them. Their most famous exploit was an annual party, and it was such an outstanding example of public debauchery that it was eventually shut down.

The First Ward Ball, which the two men organized, was referred to as an "annual underworld orgy." It was required that every prostitute, pimp, pickpocket and thief buy at least one ticket, while the owners of brothels and saloons had to purchase large blocks of them. The madams usually had their own boxes, where they could rub shoulders with city officials and politicians. The ball continued a tradition that started about 1880, when there was a charity party to honor Lame Jimmy, a pianist who worked for the renowned madam Carrie Watson. These parties continued until 1895, when a drunken detective shot another police officer at the gathering.

After the end of the charity soirées, Coughlin and Kenna took responsibility for throwing the annual affair. It grew larger every year, until the two aldermen were making as much as $50,000 from it. They held the ball at the Chicago Coliseum, and after one spectacle, the *Chicago Tribune* wrote, "If a great disaster had befallen the Coliseum last night, there would not have been a second story worker, a dip or pug ugly, porch climber, dope fiend or scarlet woman remaining in Chicago."

The 1907 First Ward Ball was perhaps the most widely reported and, for this reason, seemed to raise the most ire among the various reform movements in the city. When the ball opened that year, there were fifteen thousand people jammed into the coliseum. One newspaper reported that there were so many drunks inside that when one would pass out, they could not even fall to the floor. Women who fainted from the closeness in the coliseum were passed over the heads of the crowd to the exits.

As the event opened, a procession of Levee prostitutes marched into the building, led by Bathhouse John, with a lavender cravat and a red sash across his chest. Authors Lloyd Wendt and Herman Kogan described the parade:

> On they came, madams, strumpets, airily clad jockeys, harlequins, Dianas, page boys, female impersonators, tramps, panhandlers, card sharps, mountebanks, pimps, owners of dives and resorts, young bloods and "older men careless of their reputations."

At this point, the party really got started as women draped themselves over railings and ordered men to pour champagne down their throats.

The coliseum, one of Chicago's most famous venues, was also home to the infamous First Ward Ball, an annual orgy of sin and scandal.

The girls in peek-a-boo waists, slit skirts, bathing suits and jockey costumes relaxed and tripped to the floor where they danced wildly and drunkenly…drunken men sought to undress young women and met with few objections.

A further description of the ball included the first mention of Chicago's "drag queens" of the era, and reformers later described the antics of these men in women's costumes as "unbelievably appalling and nauseating."

Even though there had been one hundred policemen detailed to the party, there were only eight arrests and one conviction—that of Bernard Dooley, who was fined for entering the party without paying. Hinky-Dink Kenna later called the party a "lollapalooza" and added that "Chicago ain't no sissy town!"

Reform elements had attempted every year to prevent the ball from taking place but had never succeeded. After the 1907 affair, they were even more determined. In 1908, the rector, warden and vestry of the Grace Episcopal Church asked the superior court for an injunction against the event, but the court simply stated that the affair was not within its jurisdiction. On December 13, just two days before the ball was to be held, a bomb exploded in the coliseum, wrecking a two-story building that was used as a warehouse and breaking windows as far as two blocks away. The police who investigated said that it had been the work of "fanatical reformers," and the ball was given as scheduled. In fact, Bathhouse John told reporters that it was the "nicest Derby we ever had."

Reverend Melbourne P. Boynton of the Lexington Avenue Baptist Church, who apparently attended, said that it was "unspeakably low, vulgar and immoral." Public opinion sided with the minister, and the 1908 First Ward Ball was the last. When Coughlin announced plans for the event in 1909, such a storm of opposition arose that Mayor Fred Busse refused to issue a liquor license. On December 13, Coughlin and Kenna gave a concert in the coliseum, but fewer than three thousand people attended, and police were on hand to make sure that no liquor was served and that no one got out of hand. It was the dullest affair that the Levee had ever seen, and there has been no attempt to hold the First Ward Ball since.

The end came for Chicago's two most colorful aldermen not with a bang but with a sad whimper. Bathhouse John Coughlin died on November 8, 1938, an old and fading politician and a veteran of forty-six years on the city council. After all of the money he had made over the years, he died more than $50,000 in debt, thanks to gambling losses.

Hinky-Dink took care of his old friend's funeral arrangements, but there were few people around to do the same thing for Kenna when he passed on in 1946. After more than fifty years as boss of the First Ward, there were only three cars with flowers at the graveside, and the mayor didn't even attend. Unlike Coughlin, though, Hinky-Dink died a millionaire, leaving behind piles of cash (mostly in $1,000 bills), two pints of vintage 1917 bourbon, eleven suits of woolen long underwear and a 1930 Pierce Arrow Limousine. After Coughlin's death, Kenna rarely ever left his suite at the Blackstone Hotel, and toward the end, he never left it at all. He died mostly forgotten, and if not for the blatant corruption that reigned during his tenure as alderman and the debauchery of the First Ward Ball, it is unlikely that he would be remembered at all.

BIG JIM COLOSIMO

The most important criminal in Chicago during the early 1900s was Big Jim Colosimo, who ruled the underworld for a longer period of time than any man in the history of the city. The money that he raked in from the many immoral enterprises he controlled was conservatively estimated at $50,000 a month for about eight years, an enormous take at that time, although small compared with the money made by the bootleggers and racketeers of the 1920s. Colosimo was a great spender. He built a fine home for his father and an even grander one for himself, filled with an assortment of both expensive and gaudy furniture. He supported a horde of relatives, some of whom worked in his various brothels and saloons. He maintained a large staff of servants, and his two uniformed chauffeurs drove his lavish automobiles. He kept his massive girth clad in white linen suits, and he had a fixation on diamonds. He wore a diamond ring on every finger, diamond studs on his shirt front, a huge diamond horseshoe pinned to his vest, diamond cuff links and belts and suspenders that were fitted with diamonds. He bought the stones from thieves and needy gamblers and hoarded them like other men collect books and paintings. He often carried loose stones in a small bag in his pocket and, when bored, would pour them from hand to hand or would lay them out on a black cloth to watch them glisten in the light.

Colosimo was a strange character and a man who helped to usher in the era of organized crime in Chicago. He was ten years old when his father

"Big Jim" Colosimo, Chicago's first vice lord. He set the stage for organized crime in the city. *Courtesy of* Chicago Daily News.

brought him to the United States from Italy, and he spent all but two or three of his remaining thirty-nine years in the red-light districts of Chicago's South Side. He began his career as a newsboy and bootblack but quickly changed careers when he saw the money that could be made in crime. At eighteen, he was an accomplished pickpocket and a pimp, with a half dozen girls working for him. By the late 1890s, after several brushes with the law, Colosimo abandoned his life of crime and became a street sweeper, the only honest job he ever held. By 1900, he was promoted to foreman of his crew and had organized his fellow workers into a social and athletic club that eventually became a labor union. At this point in his career, Colosimo was befriended by the two most powerful political bosses in Chicago: First Ward committeeman Michael Kenna and alderman John Coughlin. Within the First Ward lay the notorious Levee District, an area filled with whorehouses, saloons and gambling parlors. Kenna and Coughlin employed Colosimo as their collector in return for the votes of all of the members of his unions.

In 1902, Colosimo married Vittoria Moresco, who ran a brothel on Armour Avenue. Within three years, the pair had established other sporting houses, and in 1910, they opened a famous café on Wabash Avenue called

Colosimo's. It became the center of Chicago nightlife, especially on the South Side. By 1912, Colosimo and his wife owned dozens of brothels, catering to all income levels. The café remained one of the most popular restaurants in the city and entertained wealthy Chicagoans, city officials and even show-business types like Enrico Caruso, the famous Italian tenor. He had also organized a white slavery ring with another resort owner named Maurice Van Bever and had acquired interest in other resorts and operations.

As one of Chicago's wealthiest Italians, Colosimo was a natural target for Black Hand extortionists. There were three different attempts made on his life, and each time Colosimo succeeded in killing his attacker. In 1909, however, he received a demand for $50,000, and this time, Vittoria convinced her husband to call John Torrio, her cousin in New York. Torrio was an Italian immigrant who began leading a gang of thugs and criminals while still a teenager. Torrio gained a reputation for viciousness. More importantly, he gained a reputation for being intelligent and quick thinking. He never carried a gun—a fact that speaks volumes about him during a time when even the lowliest street thug carried at least one weapon—because he always surrounded himself with men who carried out his dirty work. Torrio went on to own his own bar and whorehouse by the age of twenty-two, and he also got involved in local politics. In 1904, he and his gang were instrumental in the election of New York's mayor, George Brinton McClellan, stuffing ballot boxes and violently preventing people from voting for McClellan's rival.

Torrio was summoned to Chicago to help out his cousin and her husband. He dealt with the Black Hand extortionists who were threatening the Colosimos by subcontracting two gunmen, who shot them dead at the money drop.

Colosimo asked Torrio to stay in Chicago, and in gratitude for what Torrio had done, he put Torrio in charge of his empire of saloons, whorehouses and gambling dens. In 1915, he also gave Torrio permission to set up his own criminal organization. He purchased a building at 2222 South Wabash Avenue, which would be known from then on by the number of its address: the Four Deuces. The Four Deuces soon became the headquarters for a criminal enterprise far beyond anything that Big Jim Colosimo could have imagined. Within a short time, Torrio was controlling over one thousand enterprises that were all devoted to drinking, gambling or sex. His stable of gunmen eliminated anyone who opposed him.

Colosimo continued to thrive on the money that he collected from his sporting houses and saloons on the Levee, but eventually the red-light district was abolished, which turned out to be only a minor setback for Colosimo. When he realized that the segregated vice district would never be reopened, he concentrated his energies on controlling apartments and houses where prostitutes took their clients, which were usually operated in connection with saloons and cabarets. He also handled most of the protection money collected by his own and other vice syndicates, and by 1915, he was the acknowledged boss of prostitution on the South Side. Because of his political power, he was also considered to be important in other sections of the city.

Ironically, Colosimo's downfall was linked directly to his romantic interest in one of the few respectable women he had ever known.

By 1920, Johnny Torrio was looking to the future. The age of the automobile had begun, and Torrio had the foresight to see that the future of vice lay not in its traditional center but in the suburbs. The vice-ridden city had seen many reform movements over the years, but as the Prohibition era drew near, they became more effective. There were protest marches against everything from prostitution to gambling. However, it was alcohol that the protestors saw as the basis for all of this corruption, and men like Johnny Torrio knew that it was only a matter of time before the Prohibition movement managed to ban alcohol entirely.

When Prohibition finally arrived in 1920, Torrio was determined to profit from the opportunities that it presented. He soon realized that the only way for his organization to operate was by sitting down with rival gangs and marking out territory; otherwise, the battle to supply illegal liquor to the thousands of speakeasies that sprang up would lead to chaos and ongoing war. He went to his mentor, Colosimo, and presented his plans to him.

Colosimo was disinterested in Torrio's plans. By that time, he had become distracted by his romantic interest in a woman named Dale Winters, a young musical comedy actress who had been stranded in Chicago after an unsuccessful theatrical tour. She accepted an invitation to perform in one of Colosimo's establishments, and the two fell in love. In 1920, he divorced his wife and married Dale three weeks later. Torrio was astonished to find that Colosimo couldn't be bothered to protect his operations from major rivals like Roger Touhy and Dion O'Banion. This left only one solution for the problem in Torrio's mind: Colosimo had to be eliminated.

On the afternoon of May 11, 1920, Colosimo left for his restaurant with plans to meet his new wife later that night for dinner. When he arrived, he went to his office and spoke with his secretary, Frank Camilla, who had been meeting with the chef about that evening's dinner. Colosimo

Jim Colosimo and his second wife, musical comedy star Dale Winters. His attraction to her cost him his life only days after the two were married. *Courtesy of* Chicago's American.

spoke with them for a few minutes, and then, at about 4:30 p.m., he allegedly took a telephone call from Johnny Torrio, who explained that a shipment of whiskey was being delivered to the restaurant and Colosimo had to sign for it personally. Colosimo left the office and walked out in the lobby, likely preparing to step outside. A moment later, two shots were fired, and Frank Camilla went to investigate the sounds. He found Colosimo lying on the floor of the lobby with a bullet wound in the back of his head. The second bullet was lodged in the plaster wall. From the angle of the shots, the police concluded that the killer must have been hiding in the cloakroom.

The funeral of Big Jim Colosimo was held on May 15 and was the first of the gaudy burial displays that were the fashion in Chicago's underworld throughout the 1920s. Thousands attended, including both gangsters and politicians, further underscoring the alliances between the two.

Colosimo's body was discovered in the lobby of his South Side restaurant. He was shot in the back of the head shortly before Johnny Torrio and Al Capone began their rise to the top of the Chicago underworld. *Courtesy of the* Chicago Daily News.

After Colosimo's death, Torrio immediately took over Colosimo's entire operation. He had an army of between seven hundred and eight hundred men working for him, but he always had room for more. One of the soldiers that he recruited was a young man from Brooklyn whom he had known since age fourteen. In 1921, Torrio invited this man to come to Chicago and work for him. His name was Al Capone.

"SLIP HIM A MICKEY"

There are many names connected to Chicago crime that have endured throughout history, but how many of them, save perhaps Big Jim Colosimo, have been as well known for their restaurant or drinking establishment as they were for their ties to Windy City crime? There is only one other man, the proprietor of the Lone Star Saloon & Palm Garden, whose name has endured over the decades. In fact, his name has been immortalized in the American lexicon, and it is a name that has been spoken by literally thousands of people who have no idea that he was an actual person. This deadly little man, who stood only five feet, five inches tall and weighed less than 140 pounds, was Mickey Finn, and his name is now used everywhere as a synonym for a knockout drink.

Little is known about the life of Mickey Finn, but he was born in either Ireland or Peoria, depending on his mood when telling his life story. He first came to Chicago during the 1893 World's Fair as a "lush worker," which meant that he robbed drunks in the vice districts of South Clark Street. Not long after, he began working in a bar owned by Toronto Jim in the Custom House Place district but only lasted there for a few months. Finn was too tough for even this notorious hangout and was constantly fighting with customers, who were mostly hoodlums and thieves. He was finally fired after knocking out a man's eyeball with a board when the customer failed to produce the money to pay for a round of drinks he had ordered.

For the next year or two, Finn operated as a pickpocket and a fence for small-time thieves and burglars. In 1896, he opened the Lone Star Saloon & Palm Garden at the southern end of Whiskey Row. This infamous area was a stretch that ran along the west side of State Street from Van Buren to Harrison Streets, and it was where, for almost thirty years, every building was occupied by a saloon, wine room, gambling house or all three combined. A police inspector named Lavin once called the place "a low dive, a hangout for colored and white people of the lowest type." Finn ran the Lone Star for about eight years, and during most of this time, he continued handling stolen goods. He also took in money for instructing pickpockets in the "art of the lift" and taught thievery to streetwalkers, whom he encouraged to rob the men they picked up at the Lone Star.

Finn's wife, Kate Roses, also handled "house girls" for the place. They were supposed to induce the customers to drink and to entertain them in any other manner for which they were willing to pay. Two of the in-house prostitutes, Isabelle "Dummy" Fyffe and "Gold Tooth" Mary Thornton, would later be Finn's downfall when they testified against him during a 1903 vice investigation.

But the saloon's claim to fame came from Finn's novel approach to fleecing his customers. From the beginning, the Lone Star Saloon & Palm Garden (the garden was a backroom decorated with a sickly palm tree in a pot) was a robbers' den. For the first year or two, Finn and his associates contented themselves with picking pockets and rolling drunks, but they soon moved on to bigger things. In 1898, Finn met a black "voodoo doctor" named Hall, who sold love potions and charms to girls in bawdy houses and peddled cocaine and morphine to dope addicts. From the voodoo man, Finn purchased a bottle that contained "some sort of white stuff." The police never identified the substance, but it was probably chloral hydrate.

With the "white stuff" as the prime ingredient, Mickey Finn invented two knockout drinks that would become his trademark. One of them, the "Mickey Finn Special," was made from raw alcohol, water, snuff and a liberal amount of the voodoo powder. The other drink, which he dubbed "Number Two," was beer mixed with the powder and fortified with snuff water. Finn brazenly put up a sign behind the bar that invited customers to "Try the Mickey Finn Special." The house girls and whores who worked for him were instructed to push the concoction on every man with whom they drank. Finn was so proud of the drink that he named in his own honor that even the luckless customers who insisted on drinking beer only were given the "Number Two" in retaliation.

A customer who had been given one of the paralyzing potions usually quietly slumped over in his chair and slept until he could be given the proper attention by the proprietor. The bartender, or one of the house girls, would drag the man into one of the rear rooms behind the Palm Garden, which Finn called his "operating room." Finn and Kate Roses would do the actual robbing. Finn would always put on a derby hat and a clean white apron and would go to work on the man, first stripping him to the skin and searching for a money belt or anything in his pockets. If his victim's clothes were of good quality, Finn would take them and substitute rags in their place. After that, the man would be tossed into the alley out back or left on the floor of the "operating room" until the next morning. The victims were not hard to handle when awakened and were usually befuddled for a day or two afterward. Few of them ever remembered where, or when, they had been robbed.

Occasionally, however, a few of the men gave Finn problems, and he always kept a club at hand in case one started to show signs of stirring. Dummy Fyffe stated that Finn was "terribly brutal" with the men he doped, and Gold Tooth Mary later testified that things sometimes took a darker turn. "I saw Finn take a gold watch and $35 from Billy Miller, a trainman," she told the vice commission. "Finn gave him a dope and he lay in stupor in the saloon for twelve hours. When he recovered he demanded his money, but Finn had gone…Miller was found afterward along the railroad tracks with his head cut off." Mary also talked of many other men she had seen drugged and robbed in the Lone Star and explained that she had quit working in the bar in the fall of 1903 because of Finn's increasing violence.

She also reported to the commission that Finn told her that he would never be arrested because he paid the police for protection and possessed influence with corrupt aldermen Hinky-Dink McKenna and Bathhouse John Coughlin. Strangely, neither one was ever asked by the graft commission to explain or deny these boastings by Finn. Not long after the prostitutes appeared before the commission, the police raided the Lone Star but found nothing but a few bottles of liniment and some cough medicine. With no real evidence, they said, they were unable to arrest Finn. The only action the commission could take was to revoke Finn's saloon license, and on December 16, 1903, the doors of the Lone Star were closed.

Mickey Finn left Chicago for a few months but returned in the summer of 1904. He tended bar in a place on South Dearborn Street, and while he refrained from administering it himself, he sold the formula for his "Special" to a number of ambitious saloonkeepers throughout the city. To the underworld, the potion was known simply as a "Mickey Finn." To this day, his name is applied to knockout drinks of every type, earning one of Chicago's own a rather dubious place in history.

CHICAGO'S MOST FAMOUS MADAMS

The real history of the acclaimed Everleigh sisters, Chicago's most famous madams, will likely never be known. They invented and reinvented their personal backgrounds many times throughout the years, adhering to the old adage: "If the legend is better than the truth, print the legend."

What we do know is that the two sisters, Minna and Ada Lester, were born in Virginia and created the finest brothel in the world, right on the streets of the South Side Levee District, one of Chicago's most notorious crime and vice areas. The fact that they created such a fine establishment was no accident. They traveled all over the country doing careful, painstaking research and became determined to open a brothel that offered the finest luxuries and the best girls and, of course, catered to the wealthiest clients.

According to the story they passed along to biographers, the sisters were born to a wealthy attorney in Virginia in the 1870s. He sent them to finishing school to ensure that they became proper ladies, and they were quite popular on the social scene. The two of them married brothers, but neither marriage lasted, and the girls set off on a theatrical tour, eventually opening a brothel

Minna Everleigh.

Ada Everleigh.

South Dearborn Street in the Levee District. The Everleigh Club is on the right.

in Omaha with an inheritance that they received after their father died. After becoming tired of Omaha, they traveled to New York, New Orleans and San Francisco, studying what would be required to open a world-class sporting house. They eventually settled in Chicago.

The Lesters (who were to become known as the Everleighs) purchased a brothel on the south side, located at 2131–33 South Dearborn Street. The double building had once belonged to a madam named Lizzie Allen. The sisters purchased the place for $55,000 ($20,000 down, the remainder to be paid in six months, with $500 a month in rent) and received the lease, all of the fixtures and all of the working girls. Minna and Ada fired the girls who had worked for Allen and threw out the furnishings, determined to redecorate the entire house.

By February 1, 1900, the house was ready to be opened. It soon became renowned as the most opulent bordello in the city. Ada and Minna Everleigh recruited refined and cultured young women and charged their wealthy patrons as much as $500 a night for entertainment. They hired chefs, porters and servants to provide background staffing for the six parlors and fifty bedrooms located on the premises. The rooms were amazingly furnished with tapestries, oriental rugs, impressionist paintings and fine furniture, and there was even a huge library for the education of the young women who worked there. There was a waterfall in one room, and orchestras often appeared in the drawing rooms. The musicians would sometimes play all evening or musical entertainment would be provided by the club's "professor," a black piano player named Davenport Davenport, who played all of the popular tunes of the era. Occasionally, visiting musicians like Scott Joplin would be allowed to sit in for the evening.

The house was adorned with golden silk curtains, silk damask easy chairs, mahogany tables, gold bathtubs, gold-rimmed china, Irish linen and a gilded piano that had been purchased for $15,000. The rooms were equipped with fountains that periodically sprayed perfume into the air.

Meals at the Everleigh Club were as sumptuous as the décor. Breakfast for the girls, which was usually served at 2:00 p.m., often included iced clam juice, eggs Benedict, kidney pie, clam cakes with bacon, whitefish, breast of chicken, ham, buttered toast and hot coffee. The girls usually had breakfast in their rooms. Dinner, which was served at 8:00 p.m., included pheasant, capon, roast turkey, duck, quail on toast, au gratin cauliflower, spinach, creamed peas, parmesan potatoes, pear salad with sweet dressing, artichokes, stuffed cucumber salad, asparagus, candied and plain carrots with fruit and more. Dinner, like the post-midnight meal,

The world-famous Everleigh Club, located at 2131–33 South Dearborn Street. It was the fame achieved by the brothel that eventually led to it being closed down.

was served in the Pullman Room of the club, which had been fashioned as a replica of a Pullman railroad car. The late-night meal often consisted of fried oysters, Welsh rarebit, devilled crab, lobster, caviar with lemon juice and scrambled eggs and bacon.

A friend of the Everleighs, Charles Washburn, later wrote a biography of the sisters called *Come into My Parlor*. In it, he described some of the inner workings of the club, but only what the Everleighs allowed him to know. He told of how, before the club actually opened or before new girls were put to work, the prostitutes were given evening gowns and proper schooling on how to conduct themselves. Minna and Ada did not want the club to be just another brothel on the Levee. Minna instructed them:

The interior entrance of the opulent Everleigh Club.

Be polite and forget what you are here for. Gentlemen are only gentlemen when properly introduced. We shall see that each girl is properly presented. No lining up. There shall be no cry "in the parlor girls" when the visitors arrive. The Everleigh Club is not for the rough element, the clerk on holiday or a man without a checkbook.

Over the years of operation, scores of men were turned away at the door, and often no one would be admitted without a letter or card of recommendation, unless he was known to the Everleighs. The only customers who got a free pass to enter were police officers, newspaper

The so-called Japanese Throne Room at the Everleigh Club.

reporters and politicians who were in positions to do favors for the Everleighs. They already received protection from Levee enforcers like Ike Bloom and Big Jim Colosimo but knew that cops and reporters were also good to have on their side.

The sisters did not allow the girls to rob their clients, use drugs or become connected to a pimp. They had strict standards. Minna continued, "It means that your language will have to be lady-like. You have the whole night before you and one $50 client is more desirable than five $10 ones." The girls initially scoffed at the idea of earning $50 in one night, but not for long. An average client could spend several hundred dollars on the girls, and on food and drink, in a single night, and many spent as much as $1,000 during an era when a working man earned about $6 a week.

The Everleigh sisters later retired with several million dollars in the bank. If there was one key to the success of their club, it was a certain type of client. They later said, "If it weren't for married men, we couldn't have carried on at all and if it weren't for cheating married women, we could have made another million."

The Everleigh Club was the starting place of a number of Chicago stories that are still told today. One of them involved Prince Heinrich, the brother of Kaiser Wilhelm II, king of Prussia and the German emperor who visited the club during a trip to the city. During an elaborate show performed by the girls, they danced in fawn skins and tore apart a cloth bull, which thrilled the Germans.

During dinner, a historic event took place. One beautiful Everleigh girl began dancing on the table and accidentally kicked off her slipper, which struck a bottle of champagne. A gallant gentleman immediately drank from the slipper, after which each man removed a shoe of a woman sitting near him, filled it with champagne and toasted the prince, the Kaiser and "beautiful women the world over." It was the first time that champagne was drunk from a woman's slipper, and it set a new standard for cringe-inducing gallantry all over the world.

Perhaps the most dangerous story connected to the Everleigh Club involved the death of Marshall Field Jr., son of the dry goods millionaire. The younger Field had been married since 1890, but this did not prevent him from being a frequent visitor at the Everleigh Club. He lived in a home at 1919 South Prairie Avenue, and tragedy came to call there on November 22, 1905. Just before dinner that evening, Field fired a bullet into his left side while he was seated in his dressing room. The shot would eventually prove to be fatal. According to the newspapers the following morning, the gunshot had been a tragic accident. Field had been examining a loaded revolver in anticipation of an upcoming hunting trip to Wisconsin when the gun went off. It was said that it had accidentally discharged and the bullet lodged in his side, piercing his liver. Field was rushed to Mercy Hospital, where he lingered at death's door for several days.

The police were summoned to the house, and the servants were closely questioned, but no one had witnessed the shooting. Mrs. Field had been away for the afternoon. Satisfied with the "cleaning the gun" story, the police looked no further into the incident.

Marshall Field Jr. died on November 27, 1905, and was buried in a lavish ceremony at Graceland Cemetery on the city's North Side. But his death created a mystery that soon involved the Everleigh Club.

While police detectives may have accepted the "accidental discharge" story, many reporters and members of the general public were not so quick to do so. Many reporters knew of Field's frequent visits to the Levee District, and the Everleigh Club in particular, and soon rumors began to circulate that he had not really been at home when the fatal shot was fired.

Stories spread (and it was later revealed that an Everleigh prostitute was paid $25,000 by a rival madam to concoct the story) that Field had actually been shot at the Everleigh Club. The stories varied, stating that he had either been involved in an altercation in the brothel and was shot by one of the bouncers or that he was shot by one of the prostitutes when he became violent with her. Regardless, his body was then allegedly smuggled home to avoid scandal. He was later found in his dressing room, "having had an accident while cleaning his gun."

The story was, of course, denied, but not with much vehemence. Minna knew that rumors of this sort were not entirely bad for business. This is likely the reason that the story still continues to be told today by those who have a hard time believing that a pistol with two safety catches could have been fired by accident.

The Everleigh Club thrived for a number of years and was finally closed thanks to the forces of the reform movement—and a publicity campaign that somehow went awry. They were eventually shut down because of a handsome, leather-bound, privately printed booklet, which the sisters hoped would make their establishment even more famous. The booklet, which offered a tasteful write-up and professional photographs of the club, was sent out all over the country. It garnered plenty of attention for the club, but not the kind they wanted.

Mayor Carter Harrison II was said to be embarrassed by the interest that the Everleigh Club was bringing to Chicago. When visiting associates asked about the city's greatest attractions, he mentioned the soaring mosaic ceiling at Marshall Field's, the beautiful waters of Lake Michigan and the performances by the Chicago Grand Opera Company. But he was forgetting something, they said. What about the Everleigh Club?

Even when the mayor left town, the buzz about the Everleigh Club followed him. At a banquet in 1911, a young man approached him, pumped his hand and laughed, "Pretty snappy town, yours, isn't it?" The man followed that comment up with a wink and a joke about the Everleigh Club.

Soon, Harrison, who had always been willing to allow vice in Chicago as long as those who provided it kept to their place, needed to make a statement. Closing down the Everleigh Club, he knew, would do just that. The closing of the club would be the beginning of the end of the entire Levee District.

The final closing of the club, on October 11, 1911, was delayed for twelve hours because of behind-the-scenes political maneuvering. In the end, even Bathhouse John and Hinky-Dink Kenna couldn't save the place. The sisters were allowed to throw one last grand party at the club for their best customers and longtime supporters.

At 2:45 a.m., there was a knock on the door, and a police lieutenant was there to mournfully enforce the orders that he had been given. He told them, "Sorry, girls, if it was us, you know how we'd be."

Minna asked, "What do we do now?"

"Better clear out the house," he told her. "Get rid of the guests."

The crowd inside quietly gathered their coats and left. They milled around outside of the club for hours, lingering in the street and refusing to accept the idea that this night of getting "Everleigh-ed" would be their last.

But it was really over. Within twenty-four hours, the famous prostitutes of the Everleigh Club had received hundreds of telegrams and telephone calls offering them work at imitation brothels all over the country. They had to accept the offers, but most agreed that working anywhere else would never be the same. The world's most extravagant brothel was no more.

After closing, and realizing that no amount of money or connections could open the club again, the Everleighs took a six-month vacation in Europe before returning to Chicago. When they came back, they lived on the West Side for a time but decided to avoid the attention they received by moving to New York. They lived there for the rest of their lives, comfortably enjoying their earnings in the brothel business. Those who knew them never suspected what they had done in their previous life. They usually explained that the nude paintings hanging on their walls and the risqué books on their shelves had been "inherited from a relative."

Before she died in 1948, Minna was quoted as saying:

> *We never hurt anybody, did we? We never robbed widows and we made no false representations, did we? Any crimes that were attributed to us were the outcries of jealousy. We tried to get along honestly. Our business was unholy, but everybody accepted it. What of it?*

Ada followed her sister to the grave in 1960, and they were buried, side by side, in Virginia.

CHICAGO'S WICKEDEST PLACE

Home to the Everleigh sisters, the notorious First Ward Ball of Hinky-Dink Kenna and Bathhouse John and Big Jim Colosimo, the notorious South Side Levee District remains Chicago's most infamous region for vice. The Levee took shape during the Columbian Exposition in 1893, when thousands of people from all over the world descended on the city.

Visitors to the district could partake of just about every form of vice imaginable, from alcohol to women, and it became a hotbed of crime that would go on to spawn men like Al Capone, Johnny Torrio and the generations that followed them. Three vice rings formed the criminal organization that ruled the Levee and provided the area's various forms of "entertainment."

James Colosimo, an old-world Italian brothel keeper, controlled the street sweepers' union and was the first real organized crime boss in the city. After striking it rich selling the services of young women in his bordellos (one of which was named in honor of his wife), he opened a famous café on South Wabash Avenue that attracted both society patrons and gangsters to its doors. Italian opera stars often dropped in to sample Colosimo's famous pasta and to rub shoulders with dangerous Levee characters. The café was closed only twice during Prohibition and remained in business long after the proprietor was dead. Colosimo himself was shot to death inside the vestibule of his restaurant on May 11, 1920, and his garish funeral procession included three judges and nine aldermen as pallbearers. The café was taken over by Mike "the Greek" Potson, a former Indiana saloonkeeper.

The Paris, the white slavery headquarters of the vice ring operated by Maurice Van Bever. *Courtesy of the Chicago Historical Society.*

Maurice Van Bever and his wife, Julia, who operated an interstate white slavery ring that extended from St. Louis to Chicago, controlled another Levee vice ring. The ring inspired the passage of the Mann Act in 1910. Representative James Robert Mann of Illinois introduced the act that made it illegal to transport women across state lines for immoral purposes. It was believed that operators in the Levee had imported more than twenty thousand young women into the United States to work in their brothels.

Charley Maibum, who ran a pay-by-the-hour hotel where the local streetwalkers could take their clients for a quick rendezvous, operated the third vice ring. He often served as "muscle" and protection for other brothels that ran into trouble with competitors or law enforcement officials.

In addition to these, there were scores of independent operators in the district. The Levee arcade featured a number of "dollar-a-girl" joints, where the women provided services on a volume basis. Many of these unfortunate young ladies ended up on the Levee thanks to the smooth charm of oily con men, who lured them away from small-town life with promises of romance and marriage in the big city. Instead of love and excitement, they ended up robbed, beaten and "broken in" at the hellish dives of the Levee. In those days, most could see the need for organized prostitution but viewed the methods used to induce women to become prostitutes as far more unwholesome.

Chicago's Wickedest Place

In Chicago (and in every other major city of the day), vice operators had no problem paying off police officers and politicians for permission to run houses of prostitution. However, the officials were less tolerant of what was called the "procuring" of the girls, although the right amount of money could always get them to look the other way. Chicago's vice trade required so many women that procurers operated here with or without approval, and the city became a supply point for other cities in the Midwest.

But not all of the bordellos in this part of town were cheap dives filled with "white slavery" victims and broken-down old whores. It was also home to the Everleigh Club and a number of other brothels that, while certainly not the Everleigh Club, were not exactly flophouses either. Those other houses were operated by Vic Shaw, Zoe Millard and Georgie Spencer, a trio of madams who were in constant competition with the Everleighs. Shaw was a prominent red-light district fixture for almost forty years, and even after the Levee was shut down, she continued to operate brothels and call-out operations until she was well into her seventies. Millard was inclined to blame anything bad that happened in the Levee on the Everleighs and once inflicted a terrible beating on one of her girls for defending the sisters. Spencer, whose brothel was on South Dearborn Street in the same block as the Everleighs, flaunted her operation and was eventually driven out of business by the police, who usually turned a blind eye to anything that was going on. Spencer was so abrasive, however, that they refused to look the other way.

Despite the almost frantic efforts of these three madams, the Everleighs always maintained that their biggest problems came from Ed Weiss, who, with his wife, ran a brothel next door to the Everleigh Club. Weiss had married a former harlot who had worked for the Everleighs, Aimee Leslie, and the pair of them bought out the brothel next door, which had belonged to Julia Hartrauft. They remodeled the place, creating a sort of scaled-down Everleigh Club, which irritated the sisters. The success of the place was due in some part to its luxury and the beauty of the girls Weiss hired, but most of it came from Weiss's shrewdness in putting most of the Levee cabdrivers on his payroll. When a drunken spender got into a cab and asked to be driven to the famed Everleigh Club, he would be taken to Weiss's place instead. Most of them never knew the difference.

The brothel on the other side of the Everleigh Club was called the Sappho and was owned and operated by Weiss's brother, Louis. It was also a better class of resort, but it was never as popular as Ed's. There were also a number of other cheaper brothels, like the Casino, which was run by Vic Shaw's husband, Roy Jones; the Old Ninety-Two; French Charlie's; and the California, which was run by Blubber Bob Gray and his wife, Theresa McCafey. The California was one of the toughest parlor houses in the district. There were about thirty to forty girls who worked the place at one time, wearing shoes, flimsy chemises and nothing else. They stood naked in the windows and doorways whenever a policeman was not in sight, and two men worked the sidewalk outside, inviting in those who passed by. When customers appeared, the girls were brought into a large room that was empty except for a couple of benches along one wall. The girls were paraded in, and the customers were allowed to choose. The going rate for a tumble was one dollar, but fifty cents would do if the man turned out his pockets and proved that he didn't have a dollar to his name. The California remained one of the seediest dives in the district until 1909, when it was raided by federal immigration agents who were searching for foreign women who had been brought to the United States for "immoral purposes." They found six "white slaves" at the California. Blubber Bob, who weighed over three hundred pounds, tried to escape when the authorities burst in, but he got stuck in a window and it took three men to pull him out.

There were several other celebrated houses in the Levee during its heyday, including that of Frankie Wright, who called her brothel the Library. It got its name for the single case of well-worn books that graced its parlor. Big Jim Colosimo owned two large brothels in the district, the Victoria and the Saratoga. The Victoria was named in honor of Colosimo's wife, Victoria (Vittoria) Moresco. The Saratoga was managed by a New York gangster named Johnny Torrio, whom Colosimo had brought to Chicago as a bodyguard in 1908. Colosimo himself spent most of his time at his restaurant on Wabash Avenue, near Twenty-second.

At one end of the district was a notorious saloon called the Bucket of Blood, which stood across the street from Bed Bug Row. Nearby was a brothel called Black May's, which offered light-skinned African American girls for white customers and allegedly presented "animal acts" for those with a taste for such things, and the acclaimed House of All Nations, which had prostitutes from foreign countries. The place boasted a two-dollar entrance and a five-dollar entrance, although the same girls worked both sides of the house.

The Levee was a wide-open place for years, under the protection of its vice leaders, well-paid Chicago cops and, of course, aldermen Kenna and Coughlin, who made sure that the necessary money made it into the right hands. But things did not always go smoothly in this area for segregated vice.

South State Street in the early 1900s. *Courtesy of the Chicago Historical Society.*

Reformers, especially religious ones, constantly hampered operations in the Levee and eventually the crusade (and propaganda) against "white slavery" got the better of the district.

One of the most dramatic of the many attacks against the district was the invasion of the Levee by the famous English evangelist Gipsy Smith during a series of revival meetings held in the fall of 1909. On October 15, Smith announced that he planned to lead "an army of Christians" into the red-light district. He went ahead with the plan, despite the protests of police officers and religious leaders, who felt that he would only bring attention to the Levee. The evangelist replied that he actually wanted to advertise the place, that sin had to be exposed before it could be destroyed.

After his revival meeting on the night of October 18, Smith led a congregation of men, women and children, many of them wearing long black gowns and carrying unlighted torches, toward the district. Smith and his followers walked for blocks in silence, accompanied only by the sounds of trudging feet, a booming drum and the occasional jeering laugh from idlers and scoffers who stood on the street. The reformers made no effort to march in formation, and by the time they reached the Levee, reporters on hand estimated that Smith's crowd had grown to nearly twenty thousand people.

As they reached the Levee, their torches were lit and the assembly began to sing. They shuffled through the Levee in a funeral march, traversing every street and passing each brothel and bar several times. In front of the Everleigh Club, the House of All Nations and other notorious houses, the evangelist and his followers knelt in prayer. After an hour, they marched out of the district and followed Smith to the Alhambra Theatre at State Street and Archer Avenue, where the evangelist led them in a prayer service for those who had fallen in sin.

The Levee received this strange visitation in utter silence—some say an effort coordinated by the police and politicians. Brothels and saloons were closed and darkened, and the streets were nearly deserted. Even the hoodlums who formed a large procession of sightseers were strangely quiet, voicing no threats and few jeers. But within ten minutes of Smith's departure, the Levee came to life. Red lights were turned back on, doors swung open and music began to blare once more. While Gipsy Smith prayed at the Alhambra Theatre, the Levee enjoyed the biggest night in its history—and hundreds of young men who had only heard about vice in passing now knew exactly where to come to have a good time. One madam, who was interviewed by a newspaper reporter, smugly said, "We were certainly glad to get all of this business, but I was sorry to see so many nice young men down here for the first time."

The newspapers widely reported the crusade march the following day, and for the most part, their editorials dismissed it as the futile gesture of a crank. Politicians laughed, and city officials refused to comment, while ministers quickly disavowed any connection to the invasion. Vice was better controlled if it could be segregated in one place, most believed, and that way, it would not overrun the city. In the end, however, Smith's crusade had little short-term effect, but it did mark the first time that anyone had dared to launch an attack against segregated vice in the Windy City. Nothing that had happened in Chicago, not even the publication of W.T. Stead's shocking *If Christ Came to Chicago*, had so focused public attention on what was considered "the evil within its borders."

Inspired by Smith, new reform groups began public challenges against segregated vice in the city. Between the formation of the Chicago Vice Commission and the crusade against "white slavery," the days of the Levee were numbered. Embarrassment over an advertising campaign gone wrong closed down the famous Everleigh Club in 1911, and the rest of the South Side Levee only survived for another year.

A massive civil welfare parade that was organized on September 29, 1912, spurred grand jury indictments and complaints to be filed against property owners in the district. This resulted in the end of "segregated vice" in Chicago, but the Levee did not completely disappear. Many of the famous resorts from this area were bulldozed, as they stood in the way of an important east–west railroad corridor, but others remained and became the jazz clubs of the 1920s. A number of deadly occurrences still plagued the district in the years to come, but when Colosimo's was finally closed in 1945 (Mike "the Greek" was convicted for income tax evasion) and demolished in 1957, an era in Chicago's sordid history finally came to a close.

CHICAGO'S OTHER
WICKED PLACES

C hicago thrived on vice and its reputation as a wide-open town for many years. Organized vice arrived in the city before the Civil War, offering women, gambling and drink to any man who came looking for it. The Great Fire in 1871 wiped out the worst of the city's early red-light districts, but within a half decade after the rebuilding of Chicago had begun, a dozen vice districts that were even more vicious had been established. To the inhabitants and the police, they were known by colorful nicknames like the Black Hole, the Bad Lands, Satan's Mile, Hell's Half Acre and many others. Most of these areas were on the West and South Sides and became places of renown in the annals of Chicago's criminal history.

THE BLACK HOLE

The infamous Black Hole district was a group of saloons, cribs and bordellos reserved for African American customers only. They were located near Washington and Halsted Streets in the heart of a vice district that was bounded by Sangamon, Halsted, Lake and Monroe Streets. The "pride" of the Black Hole in the 1870s and 1880s was a placed called Noah's Ark on Washington near Halsted. The place was described as a "queer old three story mansion" that was once owned by Chicago alderman Jacob Beidler, a wealthy lumber dealer from a rich and devoutly religious family. The place was said to be a seething hive of corruption, with two saloons and a half dozen brothels. A former drawing room of the old mansion had been curtained off into cubicles that were just large enough to hold single cots. These cribs were rented out to streetwalkers, who charged from twenty-five to thirty-five cents to a customer for a tumble, depending on whether he removed his shoes or not. Noah's Ark became quite famous for robberies during its time in operation, thanks to the methods devised by two of the denizens of the place. One of the girls, seizing on a moment when she knew the man was completely distracted, would hold him by the arms while her partner cracked him over the head. Once relieved of the contents of his pockets, he was hurriedly deposited in the alley outside.

The largest whorehouse in the Black Hole was Ham's Place, a second-floor dive that was famous for its company of uniformed women who were always clad only in white tights and green blouses. No one knew who really owned the place, but it was believed to be an establishment under the control of Diddie Biggs, who ran another brothel on Halsted, in which the most popular girl was a midget named Julie Johnson. A member of the staff at Ham's was a three-hundred-pound piano player named Del Mason. Her husband, a thief known as Bill Allen, became a central figure in what some have called one of the most memorable incidents in the history of the Chicago Police Department.

On November 20, 1882, Allen became involved in a fight that resulted in the death of one man and serious injuries for another. Later that same night, Allen also killed a police officer named Clarence E. Wright when Wright attempted to arrest him in a shack at Washington and Clinton Streets. Allen fled to the basement of Diddie Biggs's whorehouse on Halsted and hid out there until December 3. On that day, Allen gave Julie Johnson a nickel and told her to go out and buy a newspaper for him. Instead, she informed the police of where Allen was hiding and for two dollars sold the nickel to the famous gambler Mike McDonald, who thereafter carried the coin as a lucky piece. The coin turned out to be anything but lucky for Bill Allen.

A patrolman named Patrick Mulvihill followed up on the information provided by Julie Johnson and went straight to the brothel's basement. Before he could get inside, Allen opened fire on him through a window and then fled down an alley. Help was summoned from the closest precinct station, and within a half hour, about two hundred policemen had shown up and were ripping apart the Black Hole in a search for the fugitive. Meanwhile, word spread that Allen had been flushed out and was loose, and a mob began to form. According to reports, as many as ten thousand armed men joined the police in the hunt.

Late that same afternoon, Allen was discovered hiding in a feedbox in the backyard of a house on Kinzie Street. Shots were fired, and before he could flee, Signal Sergeant John Wheeler gunned down the fugitive. Allen's body was then dumped into a patrol wagon and taken to the Des Plaines Street station. Conflicting reports started to circulate, saying that Allen had been captured instead of killed, and when the patrol wagon reached the station, it was met by an angry mob. Shouts and cries demanded that the dead man be taken from the wagon and lynched.

As the crowd worked itself into a frenzy, Captain John Bonfield and a half dozen officers frantically tried to fend off the mob with revolvers. At a break in the furor, the wagon sped into the alley next to the station, and Allen's body was shunted out of the wagon and passed inside through a window. The mob outside grew even more heated, threatening to tear down the police station, and soon it looked as though a riot was going to break out. Chief Doyle mounted a wagon and tried to quiet the crowd. He insisted that Allen was dead, but soon hoots and yells from the crowd drowned out his pleas for calm. The enraged mob members shouted that the police were concealing the killer and encouraged one another to break out the station windows and to force their way inside.

Doyle and the other officers retreated inside, and it was the chief who finally figured out the best way to calm the situation. Allen's body was stripped naked and placed on a mattress in front of the barred windows so that it could be seen from the alley. Then, Doyle and his men forced the crowd outside into a line and spent the afternoon filing them down the alley and past the window so that each of them could get a glimpse of the dead man. An eerie silence fell over this grim procession as one person after another filed past the bloody and bullet-riddled body of the black man. Not surprisingly, the crowd grew larger instead of smaller as word spread of the display. After dark, a gas jet was used to illuminate the scene, and the procession lasted all through the night and into the next morning.

Allen's body remained on display for forty-eight hours, and then, after an inquest was held, it was offered to his wife, Del Mason, for a funeral. She refused it. "I wouldn't give a dollar to help bury the stiff!" she reportedly sneered.

The Black Hole eventually faded away. The area was later industrialized and filled mainly with restaurant suppliers. Today, apartments and restaurants are located there, although several warehouses still remain.

THE BAD LANDS AND LITTLE CHEYENNE

There were few who could tell the difference between where the Bad Lands ended and Little Cheyenne began. They were both located on Clark Street between Van Buren and Twelfth, but the police considered the section south of Taylor Street to be the worst, so they dubbed that area the "Bad Lands." Police detectives described the whole stretch of Clark Street as being "about as tough and vicious a place as there was on the face of the earth."

The area was filled with saloons, dance halls and brothels, and one of the most famous characters of the Bad Lands was Black Susan Winslow, who ran a brothel in a broken-down, two-story shack on Clark Street, under the approach to the Twelfth Street viaduct. The roof of the place was level with the sidewalk, so entrance had to be gained by way of a rickety staircase. Black Susan had from two to five girls living with her, and they employed all manner of methods of attracting the attention of men passing along the sidewalk. For a long time, they would ring a sheep bell, and then they started setting off an alarm clock at regular intervals. Later (for some reason), they began tapping on the windows and hissing like snakes. Finally, they rigged up an electric battery and attached it to the figure of a woman with a hinged arm. The figure would strike the window and then swing back again, making a motion that would theoretically invite customers inside.

There were so many complaints made about robberies at Black Susan's that scores of arrest warrants were issued for her over the years. But every officer who attempted to actually arrest her returned to the station house with no idea as to how he was actually going to do so. The problem was that Susan weighed over 450 pounds and was wider than any door or entrance of her brothel. Officers often wondered how she could have gotten inside in the first place. Detective Clifton Woolridge finally solved the problem. He made it a mission to take Susan into custody, so he journeyed to her bordello in a patrol wagon, passing through an alley to the back door. After reading the arrest warrant to Winslow, who laughed at him the entire time, he removed the back door from its hinges and, using a handsaw, cut out the frame and about two feet of the wall. Then he placed two oak planks, each about sixteen feet long and a foot wide, on the doorsill and on the rear end of the wagon. One of the horses was unhitched, a heavy rope was attached to the animal's collar and the other end was looped around Black Susan's waist. At Woolridge's command, the horse lurched forward and pulled the enormous woman from her chair. She was dragged about three feet up the planks before she began to scream. Woolridge had used rough timber, and Black Susan was now pierced with splinters. Finally, she agreed to enter the wagon on her own and thundered gloomily up the planks. As they rode to the police station, Susan lay prone on the floor of the police wagon while one of her girls carefully removed the splinters from her large behind.

"After this," Woolridge later wrote, "the police had no more trouble with Susan Winslow."

Little Cheyenne was named in honor of Cheyenne, Wyoming, which was considered to be the toughest of the "railroad-end towns" that sprang up during the building of the Union Pacific line. The residents of Cheyenne were not amused by the name of the area, and in response, they began calling their own worst neighborhood Little Chicago.

Just north of the Bad Lands was a gin mill owned by Larry Gavin, and next to that was a place called the Alhambra. They were typical of the establishments in this area. The Alhambra was a place that was then called a "goosing slum," meaning that it was a small room with a low ceiling and

A row of saloons, dives and vice resorts.

sawdust on the floor. The liquor was of the cheapest sort, and it was staffed by the lowest of the area's streetwalkers. They would sit at the tables and wait for someone to buy them a drink or make a proposal for anything else.

Gavin's place was just as bad and was called "about as tough a place as you would want to visit" by a contemporary newspaperman. The newsman stated that the "rickety old chairs are occupied by females even more dilapidated…it was one of the vilest of places." The reporter took samples of liquor from Gavin's and from the Alhambra and had them analyzed. He reported that Gavin's whiskey was full of "pepper and acids" and that the Alhambra's brandy actually contained rat poison.

As bad as these places were, they were no worse than the other joints in the district, like the Pacific Garden Saloon, Concert Hall & Oyster Parlor at Van Buren Street. This place was not as high class as it sounded and was nothing more than a typical vice district dive. Later on, the place closed down and became, of all things, a religious mission. It is worth noting that it was in this mission that famous evangelist Billy Sunday was converted, decided to quit professional baseball and became a preacher. Other establishments included the fifty-cent brothels of Nellie St. Clair and Candy Molly Jones, who gave a stick of candy to every customer as a souvenir of her place. One clever newspaper writer commented that it was "probably not the only thing a patron took home from her place but those souvenirs usually lasted a bit longer."

WHISKEY ROW

The vice district known as Whiskey Row was located on the west side of State Street from Van Buren to Harrison, and for more than thirty years, every building on this stretch of street was occupied by a saloon, a wine room with girls, a gambling parlor or all three combined. Most of the places were simply thieving dens, where safe blowers, pickpockets, burglars, con men and gamblers socialized. Since just about every man on both sides of the gambling table was a cheat, there must have been some very interesting card games played there.

One of the most important operators here was an African American gambler named Mushmouth Johnson, who possessed considerable political influence in the city because he could deliver large blocks of black votes. He dominated the policy business in Chicago and ran a number of poker, faro and craps establishments. Johnson came to Chicago from St. Louis in the mid-1870s and for several years worked as a waiter at the Palmer House. In 1882, he took a job as a floor man in a gambling house on South Clark Street, and after a few years, the owner gave him an interest in the place. For years, it was known as one of the best cheap resorts in the city. It catered to players of all races, offered all games and bets as low as a nickel could be made at its wheels and tables. Johnson later sold out his interest and opened a new house at 464 South State Street. This establishment remained open around the clock for the next seventeen years. Unlike most gamblers, Johnson never bet on anything himself. Probably for this very reason, he accumulated a fortune of more than $250,000 in the saloon business. He died in 1907 with most of his money intact.

Another Whiskey Row dive keeper was Tom McGinness, who went from peddling potatoes from a pushcart to running a saloon and gambling den called the Berlin Café. Al Connolly, who was a Democratic committeeman from the First Ward for many years, also operated a saloon on Whiskey Row. During the Columbian Exposition, he served as a bail bondsman from the backroom of the place for pickpockets who got nabbed on the fairgrounds. Whiskey Row was also home to the famous Lone Star Saloon & Palm Garden, which was owned and operated by Mickey Finn, who created the knockout drink that still bears his name to this day.

Johnny Rafferty established himself on Whiskey Row in the 1890s and earned considerable newspaper notoriety for his frequent use of the expression: "I love a good thief!" In 1903, when the *Chicago Journal* called him a crook, Rafferty indignantly offered to prove that he had "never gouged out an eye, cut off a goat's tail, beaten a policeman, held up a train, or bitten off a bulldog's nose."

Andy Craig, who was a bail bondsman, politician, saloonkeeper, fence, pickpocket and burglar, was one of the more notorious denizens of Whiskey Row. In 1891, he served a four-year prison sentence for burglary, and in 1898, he opened a saloon called the Tivoli, which, he boasted, contained $8,000 worth of mirrors. The Tivoli became a meeting place for all sorts of lowlifes, and Craig served as a fence and a banker for thieves. He also became a bondsman for First Ward aldermen Kenna and Coughlin. Thanks to his political connections, he was able to get his picture and record expunged from the city's rogues' gallery, but this didn't exempt him from investigations. During a 1903 examination of graft in the police department, Craig's liquor license was revoked for flagrant violations of the law. He sold the Tivoli to Howard McPherson, a cigar maker, the following year. Craig said, "There is no use trying to do business when a lot of reformers are after you. They'll get you sooner or later." But nobody ever got Andy Craig; he died twenty-five years later, managing brothels for a new boss, Al Capone.

HELL'S HALF ACRE

The fabled Hell's Half Acre comprised an entire block that was bounded by Polk, State and Taylor Streets and Plymouth Place. It was said that every building there was occupied by a saloon, bordello or gambling den and that the area was so dangerous that police officers never entered, except in pairs—and seldom even then. The center of Hell's Half Acre's social activity was the Apollo Theatre and Dance Hall, on Plymouth Place, which was noted in the 1870s and 1880s for the masquerade balls sponsored by the brothel musicians, or "professors," as they were called at the time. The balls became so famous because at midnight the dancers would remove not only their masks but also all of their clothing. The Apollo was in existence as late as 1910, but by the late 1890s, it was frequented by mostly low-class prostitutes and their pimps.

In the middle of Hell's Half Acre was Dead Man's Alley, a narrow passage that ran from Polk to Taylor Street between State and Plymouth Place. This dark and forbidding passage was always filled with trash and scattered debris, and on one side of it were a number of abandoned carriages that were used by prostitutes. Thieves and cutthroats frequented the alley, and anyone who dared to walk through it, having no business there, was almost inevitably robbed. For more than a decade, the leader of the gang that operated in this area was a man named Henry Foster, who was better known as Black Bear. His usual method of robbery was to sneak up on a passerby from behind, wrap his massive arms around him, fling him to the ground and then rifle through his pockets.

This type of strong-arm work was done by Foster and male members of the gang, but the "brains" behind the operation was a skinny woman named Minnie Shouse, who lured men to the mouth of the alley and then divided the loot of those foolish enough to follow her into the shadows.

She was arrested more than three hundred times in a half dozen years but usually escaped punishment by returning a portion of the stolen money or by paying a policeman to threaten her victim with arrest for consorting with a prostitute. She managed to elude capture until early 1895, when she was finally sent to prison for robbing a farmer. Black Bear got into serious trouble not long after Minnie was locked up. He was hanged on July 1, 1895, for the murder of a saloonkeeper.

SATAN'S MILE

In later years, Chicago's entire red-light district was known as the Levee, and it gained its notoriety from famous operators like Jim Colosimo and the Everleigh sisters. Originally, however, the Levee name was applied only to a row of brothels, saloons and cribs on South State Street between Harrison and Taylor. It was used to indicate the toughness of the area, since levee districts in river towns were always the most disorderly locations in the community. The original Levee was part of Satan's Mile—State Street from Van Buren to Twenty-second—which also included Coon Hollow, south of Taylor Street. Most of the residents of Coon Hollow were African Americans, but there was a scattering of whites and several whorehouses with white women that were kept for the pleasure of black men. Detective Woolridge once wrote of the area:

> The tough saloons in the district were the resort of the most desperate burglars, thieves and sure-thing gamblers. Even the children here were taught to steal. Barefooted boys would rush out and jump on the foot bars of streetcars as if to steal rides, and then snatch the pocketbooks of women.

Many of Chicago's most dangerous criminals operated or made their headquarters in Satan's Mile, but few of them achieved the infamy of Kitty Adams, a strong-arm woman who was known for almost a dozen years as the "Terror of State Street." She arrived in Chicago about 1880, the wife of a pickpocket named George Shine. She left him after a few months and became an inmate of a brothel in Coon Hollow, where she learned to skillfully use a straight razor. After that, she always kept a razor concealed

One of the bordello inmates in the Coon Hollow section of Satan's Mile.

in the bodice of her dress and never hesitated to use it. She once sliced off the ear of one of her lovers, and on another occasion, during an argument with the driver of a scavenger wagon, she cut a six-inch gash in the side of one of his horses.

About 1886, Kitty established herself in a streetwalker's crib in the Levee and began her new career as a footpad, a thief who specialized in pedestrian victims. For several years, she worked with a pretty young woman named Jennie Clark, who picked up men and maneuvered them into dark alleys. There, Kitty pounced on the victim, threw an arm around his neck and, while holding his head back, threatened his neck with a razor while Jennie cleaned out his pockets.

The Chicago police estimated that Kitty committed at least one hundred robberies between the years of 1886 and 1893, when a man who was finally willing to testify against her pressed charges and she was sent to prison. But Kitty was scarcely locked behind the doors of Joliet prison when Jennie Clark began circulating a petition asking Governor John P. Altgeld for a pardon on the grounds that Kitty was dying from tuberculosis. Altgeld ordered an investigation, and when Kitty was taken before the board of pardons, she punctured her gums with a sharp object and managed to cough up enough blood that the sympathetic board became convinced that she would not live for another month. They reported their findings to the governor, and he ordered her released. Kitty returned at once to her work along Satan's Mile and was arrested several more times. The only charge the police could successfully bring against her, however, was disorderly conduct, so she was always let go after paying a small fine.

In August 1896, Kitty and Jennie were arrested after robbing an old man of five dollars. Kitty skipped out on bail, but Jennie appeared for trial when the case was called before Judge James Goggin, who was famous for his eccentric decisions. In this particular case, he ruled that any man who went into the Levee District deserved to be robbed and that the robbers should not be punished. Jennie was released, and the fugitive warrant that had been issued for Kitty was dismissed.

It took another two years for the authorities to be rid of the "Terror of State Street." In 1898, she was returned to Joliet prison, and she died there. Ironically, she perished from tuberculosis.

THE END OF
THE VICE DISTRICTS

C hicago's most famous vice district, the South Side Levee, closed for good in 1912, bringing an end to a rollicking era of Windy City crime. But the closing of the Levee did not bring an end to vice in Chicago. The bordellos and gambling parlors simply spread to other parts of the city, and many of the bars, booze girls and burlesque dancers ended up in the famed Near North Side nightclub district. This district, which received worldwide infamy for its seamy attractions, faded out of existence in the mid-1950s. The long procession of B-girls, backroom gambling, dope dealers, hipsters and strippers just seemed to vanish into the night.

Like the Levee, however, the Near North Side nightclub district did not disappear overnight. It was a slow, steady process of decline that began to fade with the advent of television. People stopped going to nightclubs to escape from their boring, everyday lives. It was easier and cheaper to open a cold beer at home and sit down in front of the television. And what wasn't killed by the acceptance of people's mundane lives died during the Daley dynasty. From 1955, the first year of Richard J. Daley's two-decade reign as Chicago mayor, up until the end in 1976, the Near North Side was forced to shed its old reputation and assume a more dignified appearance. Taverns closed down, and the Rush Street hotspots soon followed. Even Mr. Kelly's, a longtime nightclub that booked music and comedy acts direct from Hollywood, closed its doors.

Clark Street, known for its crime, vice and red-light attractions since the 1880s, also fell victim to urban renewal. Syndicate vice lords like Jimmy "the

The last of the Chicago vice districts, photographed in the late 1940s. *Courtesy of the Library of Congress.*

Monk" Allegretti and Caesar DiVarco were made to understand that in the Daley administration, sex would not be tolerated. How was this possible in a city that had created *Playboy* magazine, the "Mickey Finn," the one-way ride, the Everleigh sisters and Sally Rand's fan dance? No one could say, but it is the way things turned out. The lights went out on the Near North Side, leaving a gaping hole in Chicago's bawdy history.

Gone were the bump-and-grind hotspots like the Playhouse Café at 550 North Clark Street, which became the city's longest running "risqué show house." The outside wall of the building was pasted with photographs of scantily clad women, which beckoned to lonely men and out-of-town conventioneers to come inside and sample the attractions.

The French Casino was located at 641 North Clark Street and boasted "Chicago's largest show floor." It also claimed to have a company of well-known and beautiful girls but failed to mention that many of the men who braved the place ended up in the alley out back, dazed, beaten and with empty pockets.

The Paradise Show Lounge, at 1015 North Clark, was one of the roughest night spots in the area in the late 1950s. Captain Russell Corcoran, working for the Chicago Crime Commission, personally investigated the place in 1959. On the night he went there, he ordered a bottle of beer at the bar when he entered the place. Almost immediately, he was approached by a girl who persuaded him to order her a shot of whiskey. The girl then suggested that he come over to a booth with her, where she promptly ordered champagne, a bottle of which was twenty-five dollars. Having made it this far, the girl then offered oral sex for a price, which led to Captain Corcoran revealing his identity to the girl. He got up from the booth and, displaying his police badge, announced that the occupants of the club were all under arrest. Rather than being concerned about this, the bartender brazenly assaulted Captain Corcoran, and the police officer fled from the club.

At 1159 North Clark Street was the Talk of the Town, which bragged of having a "star-studded all-girl review, with shimmering G-strings and flimsy bras." Every conventioneer who came to Chicago dropped in at this cabaret at one time or another, but like all of the others, it is long gone, replaced by a drugstore, a faded storefront or a parking lot.

The fabulous cafés and nightclubs of Rush Street and the seedy dives of North Clark are only a memory now. They vanished like the vice districts that once made Chicago known all over the country as that "toddlin' town" and a place where anything goes—for a price, of course.

BIBLIOGRAPHY

Abbott, Karen. *Sin in the Second City*. New York: Random House, 2007.

Adler, Jeffrey S. *First in Violence, Deepest in Dirt*. Cambridge, MA: Harvard University Press, 2006.

Asbury, Herbert. *Gem of the Prairie*. New York: Alfred A. Knopf, 1940.

Bell, Ernest A. *Fighting the Traffic in Young Girls or War on the White Slave Trade*. Chicago: G.S. Ball. 1910.

Bilek, Arthur J. *The First Vice Lord*. Nashville, TN: Cumberland House, 2008.

Chicago Historical Society

Chicago Public Library

Cromie, Robert. *The Great Chicago Fire*. Nashville, TN: Rutledge Hill Press, 1958.

Demaris, Ovid. *Captive City*, New York: Lyle Stuart, 1969.

Farr, Finis. *Chicago*. New Rochelle, NY: Arlington House, 1973.

Halper, Albert. *The Chicago Crime Book*. Cleveland, OH: World Publishing, 1967.

Johnson, Curt, with R. Craig Sautter. *Wicked City*. Highland Park, IL: December Press, 1994.

Kobler, John. *Capone*. New York: G.P. Putnam's Sons, 1971.

Lait, Jack, and Lee Mortimer. *Chicago Confidential*. New York: Crown Publishers, 1950.

Landesco, John. *Organized Crime in Chicago*. Chicago: University of Chicago Press, 1968.

Lesy, Michael. *Murder City*. New York: W.W. Norton & Co., 2007.

Lewis, Lloyd, and Henry Justin Smith. *Chicago*. New York: Harcourt, Brace & Co., 1929.

Lindberg, Richard. *Chicago by Gaslight*. Chicago: Chicago Academy Publishers, 1996.

———. *Return Again to the Scene of the Crime*. Nashville, TN: Cumberland House, 2001.

———. *Return to the Scene of the Crime*. Nashville, TN: Cumberland House, 1999.

Mark, Norman. *Mayors, Madams & Madmen*. Chicago: Chicago Review Press, 1979.

McPhaul, Jack. *Johnny Torrio: First of the Ganglords*. New Rochelle, NY: Arlington House, 1970.

Nash, Jay Robert. *Bloodletters and Bad Men*. New York: M. Evans and Company, Inc., 1995.

Sifakis, Carl. *Encyclopedia of American Crime*. New York: Facts on File, 1982.

Taylor, Troy. *Bloody Chicago*. Decatur, IL: Whitechapel Press, 2006.

———. *Bloody Illinois*. Decatur, IL: Whitechapel Press, 2008.

———. *Dead Men Do Tell Tales*. Decatur, IL: Whitechapel Press, 2008.

Taylor, Troy, with Adam Selzer and Ken Melvoin-Berg. *Weird Chicago*. Decatur, IL: Whitechapel Press, 2008.

Washburn, Charles. *Come in to My Parlor*. New York: Knickerbocker Publishing, 1936.

NEWSPAPERS

Chicago American
Chicago Daily News
Chicago Herald-American
Chicago Herald & Examiner
Chicago Inter-Ocean
Chicago Sun-Times
Chicago Times
Chicago Tribune

ABOUT THE AUTHOR

Troy Taylor is the author of more than sixty books on history, crime, mystery and the supernatural in America. He was born and raised in Illinois and currently resides in Decatur, Illinois, which was called "one of the most corrupt cities in the state" during the 1920s.

Visit us at
www.historypress.net